MOVIES AND THE MEANING OF LIFE

THE MOST PROFOUND FILMS IN CINEMATIC HISTORY

by

Wayne Omura

For all the actors and actresses in the movie of my life.

Library of Congress Cataloging-in-Publication Data

Omura, Wayne
Movies and the Meaning of Life: The Most Profound Films in Cinematic History
p.cm.
Includes images.
1. Film - Criticism. 2. Philospҳy - Existentialism.

ISBN 13: 978-0-9820467-8-4

Bäuu Press
PO Box 1945
Winter Park, CO 80482

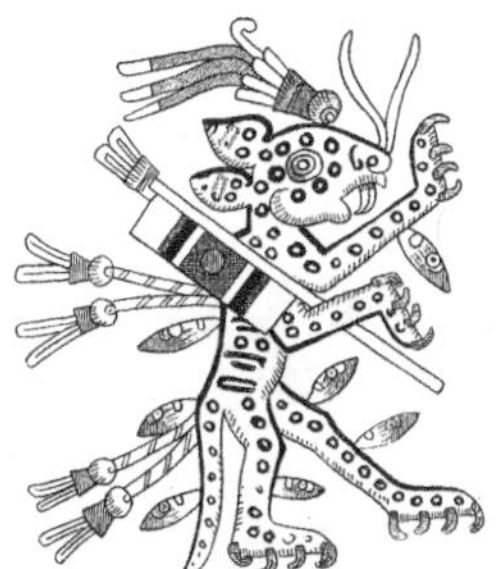

Printed in the United States of America

Contents

INTRODUCTION

The movie is a vicarious experience. It is a substitute for so-called "real" life. And yet, this illusion can move one's soul. It can place one on the beaches of Normandy with shells exploding and bullets whizzing through the air. It can place one on another planet facing alien forms of intelligent life.

In the darkness and seclusion of the theater, imagination is on par with reality. Fears, fantasies, and romances are equally accessible. With a suspension of disbelief, one can be imprisoned and tortured by a sadistic madman. One can fall in love with one's true soul-mate or engage in playful dalliances with some tart.

One can travel to distant times and places in history; meeting the greatest artists, scientists, philosophers, and leaders. Or one can project oneself into future expectations and dreams. Past and future are no longer boundaries in time. For any experience is possible in a mere two hours.

The movie is a fantasy, a distilled form of imagination. We know where we are physically in reality. But if a movie is good, our mind is somewhere else. And if a movie is excellent, our spirit has also been released. On some occasions a movie can be incredible. In such an instance our soul can be transformed. The experience of the movie can have a lasting effect on our life, transporting our spirit to a higher realm of consciousness. Yet all the while we know that the movie is only make-believe. On the other hand, from a cinematic perspective, perhaps it is our "real" life which is just pretend.

These incredibly transformative movies form the core of this book: movies that convey visions of the meaning of life. They are the most profound films in cinematic history.

Each movie falls broadly into one of eleven chapter categories. While many films may overlap categories, the most salient thematic meaning serves to differentiate.

A movie can be the most complete form of art. The cinematography is an obvious art that is mediated and appreciated by vision. But so, too, is the production design which is akin to the stage-work of a play. And costuming and make-up and special effects. All contribute to the visual aspect of a film. They are counterparts to masterworks of paintings, drawings, sculptures, and architecture. The film arts just happen to be in motion.

The soundtrack is the province of the auditory system. Whether music or sound effects or simply silence, what is heard can be comparable to a grand two-hour symphony. Songs or themes can, in themselves, become haunting melodies or even greatest hits. The sound produces the mood for the cinematic experience. It carries the tune for transporting the soul.

The plot or story line of the movie is analogous to a classic novel or an action adventure thriller. The screenplay and dialogue is comparable to a great Broadway play.

The ideas of a movie can involve the most profound concepts in history. Whether philosophical, artistic, religious, or political—the greatest thinkers of all time can win us over, either outright and blatantly, or insidiously warping our mind with subtleties combining emotion, action, and plot.

If one were to be the greatest artist of all time, one would be a director of film. But this would necessarily entail being a master creative genius on every level: musician, writer, philosopher, and artist. Perhaps only God can fill the role of the supreme artist. Perhaps life, itself, is the greatest movie, the most profound masterpiece of art.

For your entertainment: Life—the most amazing, interactive, and experiential movie of all time.

[*] Quotations not cited by footnote or attributed to an author (other than common phrases or sayings) are from the movies themselves.

CHAPTER ONE

THE EXISTENTIAL UNIVERSE

One is thrust into a seemingly indifferent universe. Forces we cannot comprehend manipulate our lives. Some are outright hostile. Others bury us in a bureaucratic avalanche of triviality. Where does the meaning lie? Is there any purpose behind it all? What significance has the individual in a world he did not create? Should we break free of the rules and structure and rebuild our own foundation? If so, what form would our new-found vision take?

THE TRIAL

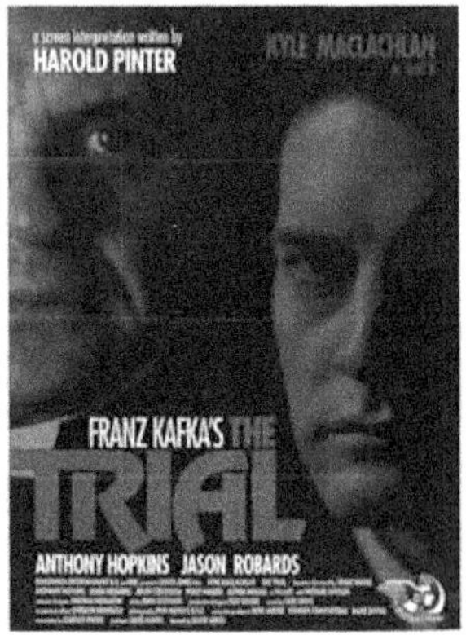

Director: David Hugh Jones
Producer: Louis Marks
Screenplay: Harold Pinter
From the novel by Franz Kafka
1992 Color

In The Trial, director David Hugh Jones and writer Harold Pinter create a film of Franz Kafka's most popular novel. It is an existential drama of man's place in society. It is a religious allegory of guilt and original sin in which the powers that be sentence man to death. But more profoundly, it is a metaphysical portrayal of man's plight in an absurd universe, a universe which he cannot possibly comprehend.

The hero of the movie, Joseph K. (Kyle MacLachlan), awakens early one morning to find himself under arrest. He is never formally charged with a crime (that may or may not come later). And he won't be imprisoned (not just yet). As for now, he may as well go about his life as usual. He can go to his job at the bank. He can even hire an advocate, for all it's worth. On the practical, mundane level it's as though nothing has even happened. It's as though merely living one's life is both the crime and the trial.

Strangeness and surreality soon begin haunting K.'s world. A hearing takes place on Sunday (so as not to interfere with his daily life). The two warders he complained about are being flogged in the broom closet of his own bank. He has an interview late at night at his advocate's home (with the advocate lying in bed). He seeks advice from a court portrait painter in a dilapidated attic studio. They are taunted by little girls who are the property of the court. When K. climbs over the bed and out a small door, he finds himself back in the hallway of the court offices. The labyrinthine court permeates everything! The trial is all-encompassing.

The bizarreness is reminiscent of a dream. And the dream begins to slowly twist into a nightmare. All K.'s attempt at a defense are frustrated and in vain, for he has no idea of the actual charge, and therefore cannot prove his innocence. All his efforts to understand the "Law" are futile, for in the end, without any actual trial, K. is evidently condemned to death.

He is taken forcibly to an abandoned quarry where he is stretched upon a boulder for execution. Two men pass a large, pointed butcher's knife back and forth over K.'s body. Then one thrusts it into his heart as they both peer, cheek-to-cheek, watching his death throes.

"Like a dog," gasps Joseph K. with his last dying breath. And so the menacing force holding sway over man's life exacts its punishment. And for what? K. was never charged with a crime. Thus he could never offer a defense. The crime of living? Original sin? The offense of being a man? Was he already guilty from the very start?

And so, the insidious force controlling life reveals itself for what it is: a murderous band of sadistic cutthroats, a nightmare horror inimical to man. It is interesting to note that what Kafka posited as the insidious nature of reality was actually vindicated through the living example of Kafka's own life. After many years of continual suffering, he died as a result of tuberculosis or consumption—a wasting away of living tissue, a deterioration which, in effect, literally consumed him alive. Fortunately Kafka died before the crisis which overtook his family. For, almost as though in confirmation of his paranoid pessimism, all three of his sisters came to the same fate as Joseph K.: exterminated like rats in Nazi death-camps.

> "Like a dog!" he said; it was as if the shame of it must outlive him."[1]

1. Franz Kafka, The Trial (New York: Alfred A. Knopf, Inc., 1956), p. 286.

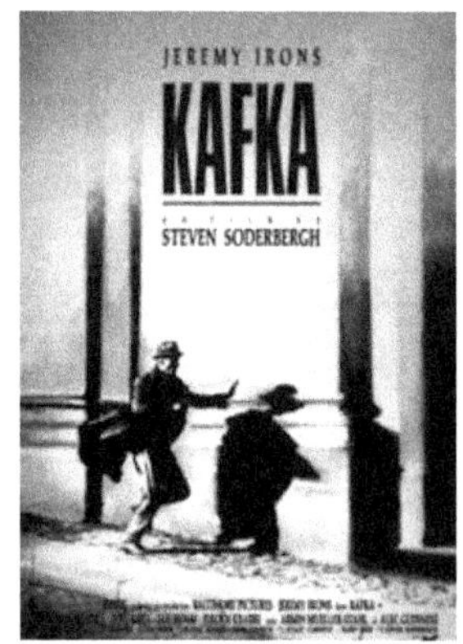

KAFKA

Director: Steven Soderbergh
Producer: Stuart Cornfield & Harry Benn
Screenplay: Lem Dobbs
1991 Color/B & W

In Kafka, Steven Soderbergh and Lem Dobbs create a masterful blending of Franz Kafka's fiction with his real life. Characters and situations are taken from both novels and stories. But the basic structure relies mostly upon a loose interpretation of The Castle. Filming is true to form, being shot in old Prague which is Kafka's home town.

The plot of the movie is Lem Dobbs creative fantasy. Kafka (Jeremy Irons) is an insurance clerk in a large firm. One day he notices his friend and close associate, Edward Raban, is missing. He investigates, and the police tell him his friend's body was found in the river. Suicide? At first Kafka believes so, but Gabriela Rossman, another co-worker (who was Edward's lover), tells him that Edward had been summoned to the Castle on the night he disappeared.

Kafka becomes suspicious. It turns out that Gabriela is a member of an anarchist group who meet secretly, throw bombs, and plot to undermine the Castle authority. They believe the Castle and its underlings are ruthless murderers. They are convinced Edward was a victim of their evil machinations since he was secretly a member of their group.

Meanwhile, Kafka is given Edward's promotion, as well as two bumbling assistants. As he investigates further, he believes there is a malevolent conspiracy. Gabriela goes missing under suspicious circumstances. But the real horror begins when the Castle kills off most of the anarchists, and quickly and surreptitiously removes their bodies.

Kafka's two assistants forcibly abduct him. They are agents of the Castle taking him off for no good. But Kafka is rescued, at the last minute, by his friend Bizzlebek, the gravedigger. Kafka then decides to sneak into the Castle from underground and plant a bomb. He also wants to find out what all this secrecy and intrigue is about. Why was Edward murdered? Where is Gabriela? Is there some nefarious purpose behind the workings of the Castle?

Kafka is discovered by the leader, Dr. Murnau, who brags about his secret experimentation. Kafka will die anyway, and so there is no harm in him knowing. Besides, Murnau feels Kafka is a kindred spirit. Kafka disagrees: "I've tried to write nightmares, and you've built one."

It turns out that Dr. Murnau and his team of scientists are cutting open the skulls and brains of living victims in order to find out the secret of human nature. He wants to create more efficient human laborers, so he must know what sets people apart. He can then engineer humans to be more productive for the Castle.

Kafka is appalled. The horror is akin to a trip through Frankenstein's Castle. The timely bomb goes off and Kafka is able to escape. When he returns to normal life, it is as though nothing has even happened. The Castle authorities, who control the police, want to make sure Kafka won't talk. The police show him the body of Gabriela who was murdered in the Castle.

"We are recommending, for the report, a verdict of suicide.
What would be your opinion?" asks the inspector.

"Suicide," says Kafka sheepishly.
"I'd have to agree."

Back at his insurance firm, Kafka is greeted by his assistants who had tried to kill him the night before. All is forgiven?—as long as Kafka makes no more waves.

Director Steven Soderbergh successfully depicts his own version of a Kafkaesque nightmare. In the light of day, the world of commerce, politics and daily life seem to govern. At night the truth unfolds with vicious murder, sadistic torture, sinister plots, and dastardly deeds. One must agree to all this if one wants to secure one's position in the Castle hierarchy. It is Kafka's own surreal vision of the cosmic order gone mad.

WOMAN IN THE DUNES

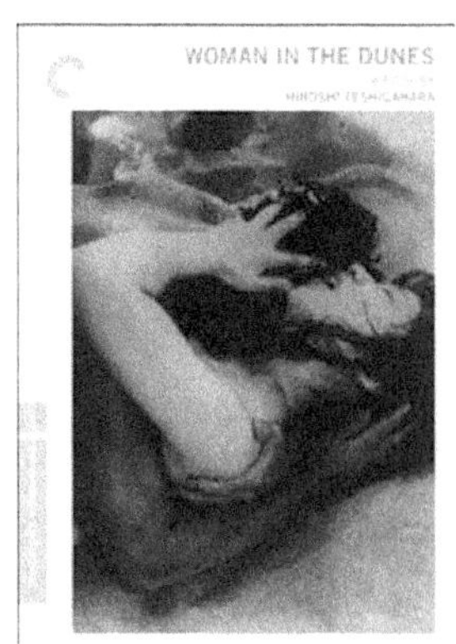

Director: Hiroshi Teshigahara
Producer: Kiichi Ichikawa & Tadashi Ono
Screenplay: Kobo Abe
From the novel by Kobo Abe
1964 B&W
Japanese with English subtitles

How many of our limitations are self-imposed? Is true freedom an abstraction which none of us really want? Writer Kobo Abe and director Hiroshi Teshigahara explore these questions in the bizarre, existential masterpiece Woman in the Dunes.

The movie begins with entomologist, Jumpei Niki (Eiji Okada) on a three-day holiday exploring the sand dunes along the coastal countryside. He is looking for a particular tiger beetle which may get his name immortalized in the insect world.

While wandering about and enjoying himself, he overlooks the time. It is getting late, and the last bus for town has already left. Villagers find shelter for him in an old, wooden shack occupied by a young widow. The shack is at the bottom of a sand pit quarry—like the miniature inverted cone of a volcano. The only way down is by a rope ladder or by a pulley that lifts sand and lowers supplies. The man is grateful that he has somewhere to spend the night. He climbs down willingly to his fate.

The woman is nice and considerate. She cooks dinner, serves tea, and fans him while he eats. Later, she goes out to load sand onto the lift. He offers to help, but she says ominously: "No, not on your first day." He laughs it off, "I'm only staying tonight." But it turns out he is wrong. He is being held captive for forced labor, although he hasn't yet a clue.

In the morning he goes outside to leave, but the rope ladder has vanished. He is trapped! He tries to climb the steep sandy walls, but they just crumble and collapse. He is at the mercy of those above.

The sand pit is eerily reminiscent of the conical pits that ant lions make to trap their prey. When an unwary ant stumbles at the edge of the pit, it falls and sinks to the center. Every attempt to climb out causes an avalanche of sand to cascade down, sliding the ant closer to the center of the pit. The ant lion lies in wait. With the struggling and flailing of the ant, he emerges from the center, attacks and consumes.

At the center of the sand pit stands the shack. The ant lion is the woman. The man is the struggling ant.

The man rebels against his imprisonment. He ties up the woman so she knows how he feels. He refuses to work, or allow her to work. The result: the villagers no longer send down food or water. Water is the most crucial. They begin dehydrating and dying of thirst. "If we start working . . ." says the woman. The man gives in. They shovel sand. They get water.

Day by day goes on the same. The man is looking for a way to escape. He secretly makes a rope and a grappling hook. He is shocked by the woman's acceptance of this way of life. "I don't understand. Doesn't this fill you with emptiness? Are you shoveling to survive, or surviving to shovel?"

The man makes a break for it while the woman is asleep. The grappling hook works. He climbs outside onto the dunes. The villagers are in hot pursuit. The man stumbles along the seashore and, in the darkness, falls into quicksand. He has no choice but to call for help. The villagers return him to the woman in the pit.

The man resents his captivity, being forced to labor so that others can profit from quarrying sand. He learns that others are being held prisoner in other pits: a student, a postcard salesman. The man continues to make plans for escape. He tries trapping crows in a pitfall sand-trap. If he is successful he will be able to tie a note to their legs. Eventually someone might find a note, if he traps and releases enough crows. "This is absurd. I won't die like a dog! I won't!"

But as the days and months go by the inevitable happens: the man and woman become intimate. Was this the plan all along? Is this why he was paired with a woman? A veritable forced marriage? Well, it works. And the villagers want to watch. They agree to allow him an hour a day of freedom up above, but only if the two perform intercourse for all to see. The man considers his situation and decides to go along. "We're pigs anyway."

But the woman will have none of it. She fights the man off as he attempts to rape her in public. The crowd goes wild, pounding drums in festivity.

Eventually nature takes its course. The woman becomes pregnant, and is taken away to the doctor. In all the commotion no one notices that the rope ladder is down. When everyone is gone, the man climbs out and wanders along the seashore.

The most shocking scene comes when the man uncovers a pitfall sand-trap that is filled with water. In the reflection of water there is an image, a figure. As the water stills, a man is looking down from the cliff above. It is the man's own pitfall sand-trap for catching crows! He is at the bottom of the pit. He has voluntarily returned to his own prison!

He thinks to himself that he has time later to escape. Meanwhile, he is eager to tell others of his inadvertent invention of a dune-still for condensing water out of moist sand.

The conclusion is shocking. Kidnapped. Forced labor. Sexual humiliation by an entire village of voyeuristic perverts. And when he has a chance to escape, what does he do? He returns voluntarily to his cage, fooling himself into believing that he can always escape later.

Kobo Abe and director Hiroshi Teshigahara have created a parable parody of modern life. Man complains about his fate, but willingly accepts all the restrictions set upon him by society and culture and his own fear of being free. One can almost imagine the entomologist prisoner as now being happy. Happy that he'll now raise a family of slaves in a shack that will be their tomb and a sand pit that will be their grave. Is Woman in the Dunes an allegory for man's plight in an absurd universe?

HEART OF DARKNESS

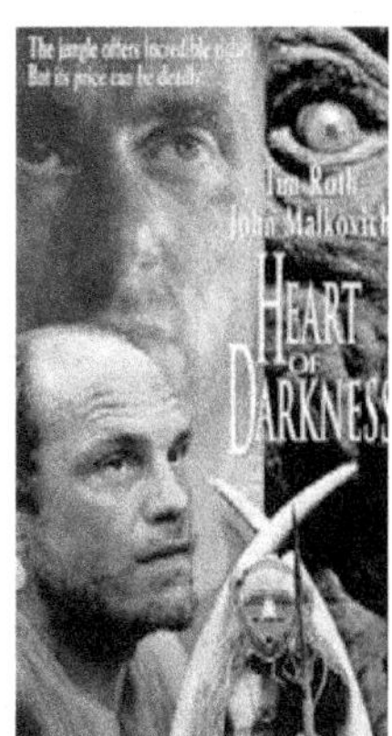

Director: Nicolas Roeg
Producer: Bob Christiansen & Rick Rosenberg
Screenplay: Benedict Fitzgerald
From the novella by Joseph Conrad
1994 Color

What if this world is pure evil? What if society is based upon greed and lies? What if nature is red in tooth and claw? And there is nothing more to existence but "the horror!" The Gnostics believe life on earth was created by a demon. Director Nicolas Roeg ponders these imponderables as he fleshes out Joseph Conrad's profound story, "Heart of Darkness."

The movie begins with Captain Marlow (Tim Roth) being hired by a Belgian Trading Company. His task is to travel into the Belgian Congo, up river to a trading post that has cut off supplies of ivory. The head of this innermost, isolated post is Kurtz (John Malkovich). Rumor has it that he's gone mad, and is sitting on a hoard of ivory. The natives worship him as a god, but he is in bad health and possibly dying.

Marlow's mission is to travel by steamboat up river, reestablish contact, ascertain Kurtz's condition, and renew the flow of ivory. But such a straight forward mission begins ominously. The company doctor remarks, "The changes take place . . . inside . . . Is there any madness in your family?"

Captain Marlow and his crew are like pilgrims venturing into the heart of the darkest continent in the world, the darkness within the heart of man's soul, and the universal darkness within the heart of all life. The darkness is everywhere. Even Marlow's head native, Mfumo, admits to being a cannibal. The savagery is hidden by only a thin veneer of civilization. But at least Mfumo is true to his nature and honest about his intentions.

Society, on the other hand, so-called civilization, spouts ideals, but only to hide their greed. Under the guise of civilizing these savages and spreading Christian virtues, natives were enslaved and starved, the continent plundered, for all that really mattered was the bottom line. "It's just robbery with violence.

Aggravated murder on a great scale." The quest for ivory veiled by ivory-tower idealism—the phrase carries a double-edge. The idealism was in fact the idealization of the ivory.

Marlow himself is an idealist, just as was Kurtz. But the heart of darkness changes all that. After seeing the ruthless exploitation, the violence of man's nature, the savagery of the jungle—ideals begin to wear thin. Any honest person cannot maintain the lie.

Kurtz was the emissary of humanity in its attempt to civilize a barbarous world. He was writing a report and guideline for the "International Society for the Suppression of Savage Customs." However, he ends his report (after his corrupt transformation) with the clear and simple words: "Exterminate all the brutes!"

Captain Marlow and his pilgrims continue their journey. They are attacked by Kurtz's natives, and Mfumo the cannibal is killed. The natives are afraid the steamboat has come to take Kurtz away. They cannot bear to lose their god incarnate.

Marlow meets Kurtz. He soon realizes why the natives worship him as a god. He is the pure embodiment of savage, capricious power. He does whatever he wants, kills anyone at a moment's notice. No remorse. No regrets. He has no conscience. He has become inhuman. He acts just like a god. He is like nature. He is the world. He is the jungle. "Why, he's mad."

Marlow has the opportunity to witness a god in action. While talking peacefully inside the hut, a pet monkey scampers about, climbing into the arms of Marlow, and then Kurtz. Without warning, Kurtz calmly and serenely twists and cracks its neck, letting the body slump to the floor. No reason. Just a whim.

In another instance, the pilgrims are attempting to load the hoard of ivory. It's really no use to Kurtz since he is dying anyway, but just out of malicious godliness, he offers an inhuman barter. "For the boys exchange I will allow half the ivory to be shipped back. Take it. Take it away quickly before I change my mind." The Belgian trading agents readily agree. Marlow is incensed, but he can do nothing. The natives far outnumber and can overpower him, especially when even his own men are on their side.

Kurtz orders one of the boys to be sacrificed. His head and hand are soon on display, mounted on a pole outside Kurtz's hut.

Kurtz eventually dies, and in the confusion Marlow and the others are allowed to escape. Marlow orders the crew to leave the ivory, for he knows at what cost it was obtained. It was a bargain made with the Devil. Not only the native boy—word has it that Kurtz raided and plundered and killed to obtain the vast hoard. Marlow knows the ivory is the motive for pillaging the heart of darkness. It is the direct cause of so much savagery.

Kurtz has discovered that the reality of the universe and the truth of man's being lies solely within the darkness of liberated animalistic instincts. Senseless murder, wanton depravity, sadism, torture, lust and greed—all are the exclusive province of the ultimate Absolute. At the heart of reality is pure horror and evil. During a brief moment of lucidity as Kurtz lies dying, his last words of judgment as he cries out at some image, at some vision . . . "The horror! The horror!"

Marlow returns to civilization and gives his narrative report. The words of Kurtz haunt him as he wanders the streets of society: "Remember, there is no more empty nor detestable a creature in nature than the man who runs away from his demon."

Kurtz had embraced his demon, and was idolized and adored. But Marlow, seeing the same reality, condemns Kurtz's world-view as "the center of abomination."

Director Nicolas Roeg ends the movie with Kurtz's haunting admonition not to flee one's demon. Whereas Joseph Conrad ends his novella with a slightly more encouraging view.

Marlow acknowledges the horrible nature of reality, and yet resists it until his last dying breath, with the ascetic discipline of Stoic defiance, outside and aloof from human life—a cold, stern judge who knows the somber gravity of the truth.

> Marlow ceased, and sat apart, indistinct and silent, in the pose of a meditating Buddha. Nobody moved for a time. . . . The offing was barred by a black bank of clouds, and the tranquil waterway leading to the uttermost ends of the earth flowed

somber under an overcast sky—seemed to lead into the heart
of an immense darkness.[1]

---

1. Joseph Conrad, Heart of Darkness (New York: W.W. Norton & Company, Inc., 1963), p. 79.

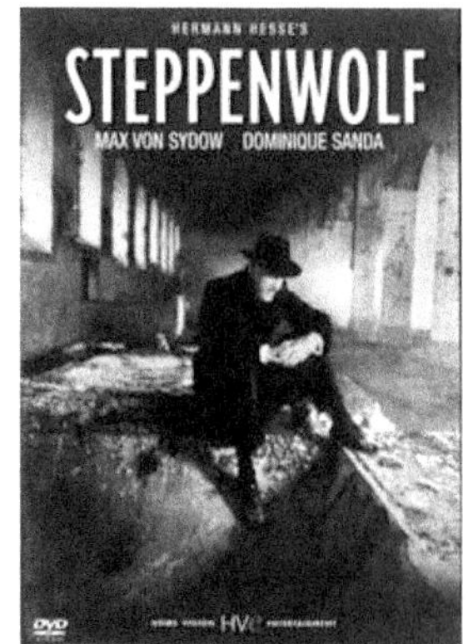

STEPPENWOLF

Director: Fred Haines
Producer: Melvin Fishman & Richard Harland
Screenplay: Fred Haines
From the novel by Hermann Hesse
1974 Color

How can one seriously pursue transcendence, and yet not lose one's sense of humor? Too often, the spiritual seeker is a grim critic of himself and others. He doesn't know how to laugh. Director Fred Haines and Nobel prize-winning writer Hermann Hesse portray the pathos of a soul-searching author bent on self-destruction.

The main character, Harry Haller (Max von Sydow), fancies himself an old steppenwolf. He feels himself to be an alienated martyr for truth. He suffers from gout, loneliness, and a sense of meaninglessness. Despondent over life, he has arbitrarily set his fiftieth birthday as the date of his impending suicide.

Harry's problem is that he takes life too seriously. Rather than enjoying and affirming with lighthearted gaiety, he insists on mulling over the problem of existence. And yet he fails to come to terms with the nature of life. Neither does he come to terms with the nature of his own self. Thus he is trapped in the vacuum of an existential void.

To be sure, Harry has glimpses of the divine through Goethe and Mozart and the timeless realm of the Immortals. But his gravity constantly draws him down into the world of bourgeois meaninglessness. He cannot yet exist in the rarefied atmosphere of the eternal. His subsequent disillusionment results in a bleak and pessimistic Weltanschauung, a nihilistic restlessness and denial of the human spirit. Hence, the "Steppenwolf Syndrome."

Harry's lack of faith in the Immortals causes him to vacillate between the polarities of the divine and the animal, an oscillation which catches him in the middle-ground of the bourgeoisie. Rather than accepting with levity this superficial realm of contradictions, Harry's seriousness drives him to the brink of suicidal despair. As the Steppenwolf, he is floundering in the tepidness of a bourgeois hell when he meets his Jungian anima, Hermine (Dominique Sanda), a high-class courtesan who frequents the jazz clubs. Hermine liberates the lone wolf by showing him how to have fun and to dance—to forget his troubles and to delight in the mere appearances of life. She also introduces her friend, Maria, who teaches Harry the joy of physical love.

Harry begins to understand when Pablo, a jazz saxophonist, introduces the "Magic Theatre." Its myriad doors and strange mirrors, as well as the psychedelic concoctions of Pablo's mind-altering drugs, reveal the comical transience and flux of so-called "reality." Life is not what it seems. The world is not how it appears. Life is a universal game—a process, not a goal. Everything is revealed as only apparent manifestations. Harry can thus envision and play reality however he pleases, for Mozart and the Immortals demonstrate the method of seeing through the appearance, penetrating the masks and illusions with the visionary spectacles of humor. As Pablo maintains, "There is a light within. You need only step out of your own shadows to see it."

Harry emerges from the Magic Theatre, and from the Hell where he met and killed the image of Hermine. He finally realizes that the world is a playground of infinite mutability, an ever-changing tapestry of meaning and light.

At his cosmic trial for killing Hermine, and thus taking the Magic Theatre too seriously, Harry is condemned to eternal life. He is also sentenced to be laughed out of court. The Immortals begin laughing, and Harry joins the symphony of cosmic laughter. His joyous figure is superimposed against the clouds and sky as the universal understanding dawns. He had spent half a century taking himself and the world too seriously. Life's purpose is affirmation, not denial. Life was meant to be enjoyed with childlike exuberance and humor. The laughter is thus the philosopher's stone, and the secret of transcendence.

This is the lesson which Harry promises to learn: that life is a game to be played and enjoyed. Rather than mulling over the rules, the contradictions and discrepancies, Harry must delight in spontaneity and childish simplicity. For only thus can he see beyond the distorted radio music of life—the earthly static behind which plays the Handelian concerto, the cosmic melody and harmony which is the essence of the eternal. Harry perceives and is saved. The way to transcendence is to cosmically laugh at the apparent absurdity and madness, the distortions and strident discords of human existence. Or as Pablo remarks in the guise of Mozart, "Learn what is to be taken seriously, and to laugh at the rest."

Director Fred Haines and writer Hermann Hesse have themselves created a playful masterpiece. What Steppenwolf reveals is that life is ultimately analogous to a "Magic Theatre" or dream—a metaphysical playground where anything and everything can, if dreamt with sufficient laughter, eventually come true. Life is hence a joke with transcendence as the punch line. It is an infinitely subtle game played solely by Immortals.

> "I understood Mozart, and somewhere behind me I heard his ghostly laughter.
> I knew that all the hundred thousand pieces of life's game were in my pocket.
> A glimpse of its meaning had stirred my reason and I was determined to begin the game afresh. . . .
>
> One day I would be a better hand at the game. One day I would learn how to laugh.
> Pablo was waiting for me, and Mozart too."[1]

---

1. Hermann Hesse, Steppenwolf (New York: Holt, Rhinehart and Winston, 1957), p. 243.

I HEART HUCKABEES

Director: David O. Russell
Producer: David O. Russell, Gregory Goodman
& Scott Rudin
Screenplay: David 0. Russell & Jeff Baena
2004 Color

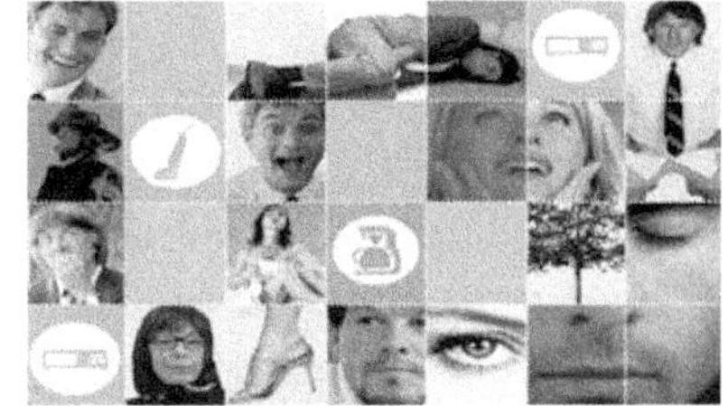

Is everything mystically connected? Are we one with all? Director/writer David G. Russell and writer, Jeff Baena believe the universe is a harmonious whole. We are one, even with the dark side, the emptiness, the void, the evil, the existential nausea.

I Heart Huckabees is a whimsical, metaphysical comedy about the search for identity and meaning in a materialistic, ever-expanding society. Albert (Jason Schwartzman) is an environmental activist, founder of the Open Spaces Coalition. His life is a mess. He's dealing with political in-fighting in his group. And he doesn't know whether anything he does is worthwhile.

By chance, he encounters the same African man three times in different places. It can't be sheer coincidence. There must be some meaning behind it all. He takes the synchronicity as a sign of higher things to come.

By chance, Albert also discovers the existence of an existential detective agency. He makes an appointment to find out what's wrong with his life. He wants to understand what it's all about. At first, Vivian (Lily Tomlin), one of the owners and investigators of the agency, attempts to dissuade Albert from his quest:

> Mr. Markovski, we see a lot of people in here who claim they want to know the ultimate truth about reality. They want to peer under the surface at the big everything . . . but this can be a very painful process full of surprises.
> It can dismantle the world as you know it.
> That's why most people prefer to remain on the surface of things.
> Maybe, you should go home. Let sleeping dogs lie. Take it easy.
> What do you say?

But Albert insists. He is adamant. He wants to know the truth at any cost. And so Vivian agrees to take his case pro bono. She and her husband, Bernard (Dustin Hoffman), will trail him through his daily life to uncover his metaphysical problem. They will scrutinize every aspect of his life. For "there's nothing too small . . . If we might see you floss or masturbate . . .that could be the key to your entire reality."

As a prelude to their investigation, Bernard introduces Albert to his "Theory of Everything." Bernard is the "therapeutic philosopher" who believes the universe is like a blanket. All the matter and energy, everything that exists in all its possible forms, is just a protrusion in the blanket of the universe. Because of this, everything is interconnected.

We are the world, for we are the blanket. It's simply a different manifestation of the essential oneness. Albert is intrigued: "Everything is the same even if it's different." "Exactly," says Bernard:

> But our everyday mind forgets this.
> We think everything is separate.
> Limited. I'm over here. You're over there. Which is true. But it's not the whole truth because we're all connected. . . .O.K.? . . . now, we need to learn how to see the blanket truth all the time.
> Right in the everyday stuff.

Albert must practice meditation on the "blanket theology." Like Charlie Brown's Linus, it will make him feel secure in an existentially-threatening universe.

Tom (Mark Wahlberg) now enters the picture as another client of the existential detectives. He's having a crisis. His wife is leaving him because of his nihilistic philosophy. She realizes it can never work because: "If nothing matters, how can I matter?"

Tom explains his metaphysical crisis to Bernard: "So if this world is temporary— identity is an illusion— then everything is meaningless . . ." Tom had gotten these ideas from a book by Caterine Vauban, a former pupil of Bernard and Vivian. Caterine had broken away from their "wholeness" doctrine and developed a nihilistic school of thought of her own: "nothing's connected, doesn't matter what you do . . ."

Enter Brad Stand (Jude Law), an executive at Huckabees (a mega-department-store chain). Brad is working with Albert's Open Spaces Coalition as a public relations move to improve the image of Huckabees. But Brad soon becomes interested in the Coalition as a way of sleeping with the enemy. He vies for leadership, and quickly becomes Albert's arch-nemesis. For he is everything Albert isn't. He's popular, handsome, successful, and a natural-born leader. He eventually wrestles control of the Coalition from Albert, who is kicked out of the organization that he, himself, founded.

Albert now meets and forms a buddy-system link with Tom. They are both clients of the existential detective agency, as well as committed environmentalists. Through Tom, Albert meets Caterine Vauban and learns her philosophy: "Betrayal embodies the universal truth you seek. Cruelty, manipulation . . . meaninglessness." Albert is tempted toward the dark side.

The two philosophies clash: wholeness or the void—with Albert, Tom, and Brad caught in the middle. Brad had also become a client of the existential detectives. By the end of the movie the world is topsy-turvy. Popular Brad loses his job, his house, his girlfriend. But now Albert can identify totally with the loser, because he is one himself.

In an epiphany, Albert realizes that we are all connected, but at the same time, everything is also meaningless and void. It is like the yin and yang: two complementary principles that need each other to be whole. It embodies the popular belief that "opposites attract" or that "you need pain and suffering to appreciate happiness and pleasure." Somewhat trite and "new-agey," but an interesting premise for a metaphysical light-comedy.

CHAPTER TWO

THE SEARCH FOR UNDERSTANDING

Some would give anything for a glimpse of eternal truth. To them, nothing else matters but the pursuit of knowledge and wisdom. Everything else is merely a frivolous distraction. But the search becomes obsessive.

The seekers are considered to be fanatics, lunatics, and eccentrics. And yet, the understanding they have garnered—is it paranoid delusion or creative genius?

Another possibility is that they have grasped the philosopher's stone, the Holy Grail, the trees of knowledge and of life.

FAUST

Director: Jan Svankmajer
Producer: Jaromir Kallista
Screenplay: Jan Svankmajer
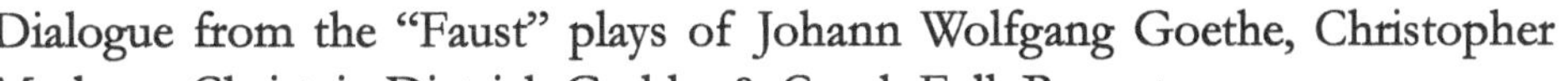
Dialogue from the "Faust" plays of Johann Wolfgang Goethe, Christopher Marlowe, Christain Dietrich Grabbe & Czech Folk Puppeteers
1994 Color

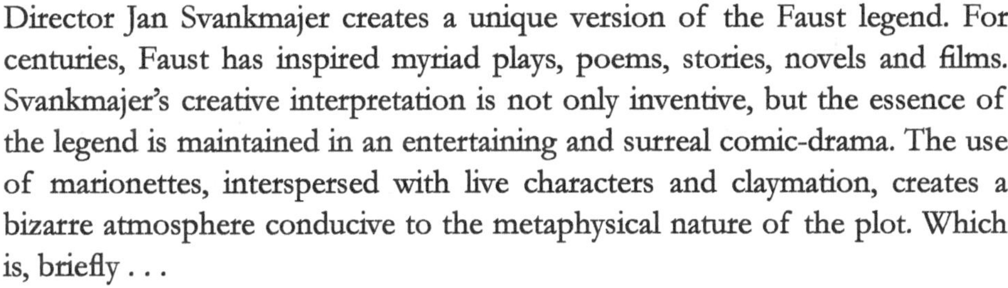

Director Jan Svankmajer creates a unique version of the Faust legend. For centuries, Faust has inspired myriad plays, poems, stories, novels and films. Svankmajer's creative interpretation is not only inventive, but the essence of the legend is maintained in an entertaining and surreal comic-drama. The use of marionettes, interspersed with live characters and claymation, creates a bizarre atmosphere conducive to the metaphysical nature of the plot. Which is, briefly . . .

Faust (Petr Cepek) wants knowledge and power. To obtain them he is willing to give anything, even his soul. With ritual incantation he summons Mephistopheles. Faust proposes to give up his soul after twenty-four years if Mephistopheles will be at his beck and call—giving him anything he desires, revealing to him whatever he chooses to know.

After a quick consultation with Lucifer, Mephistopheles returns and agrees to the bargain. A contract is drawn up and Faust must sign it in his own blood. He does so and Mephistopheles' servitude begins. Time passes quickly, in fact too quickly. Mephistopheles has tricked Faust by serving only twelve years instead of twenty-four. For he was called into service both day and night, double-duty, so the time is halved.

Lucifer comes to collect Faust's soul, and no one can stop him, for he is all-powerful. Faust is chased into the street where he is run down by a car and dies.

All this follows the basic Faust legend (except the car). But Svankmajer introduces an interesting philosophical premise. Faust is dismayed by the limits of what Mephistopheles has revealed. He wants to know everything. But Mephistopheles says, all Faust can know is what words can describe. The nature of language limits the knowledge Faust can understand.

> " . . . I seek the reason governing life's flow, and not just its external show." . . .
>
> "They lie outside the boundaries that words can address. And man can only grasp those thoughts which language can express."
>
> "What? Do you mean that words are greater yet than man?"
>
> "Indeed, they are."

Mephistopheles cannot reveal what man has no words for, because man's conceptual mind is limited by what can be described. This is an amazingly profound statement coming out of the mouth of a claymation puppet head. Another interesting mechanism of Svankmajer, is the interchanging of life-sized puppets with real characters. Only in the theater are the marionettes seen for what they are. When they go outside the theater they usually disguise themselves in large, upturned overcoats and bulky pants and hats. Even Faust is enclosed inside a wooden marionette when he agrees (inside the theater} to sign a pact with the Devil. To go outside, into the real world, he must first take off his mask.

Svankmajer seems to be saying that in the metaphysical realm of the theater, we are only puppets to the cosmic battle between heaven and earth, good and evil. In the so-called real world, we at least appear to be free. Or so it seems. Who knows if Lucifer wasn't driving the car that ran down Faust! For when the door opens, there is no driver.

The legend of Faust is the drama of man's soul torn between good and evil, struggling for power and self-enhancement. It is the story of man's quest for understanding, a grasping and biting of the apple from the Tree of Knowledge. And just as with Adam and Eve, Faust loses his innocence and is subject to damnation. With Eve it was the Serpent. With Faust it is the Devil.

Corruption in exchange for knowledge and power is a classic theme, a universal archetype in man's psyche and soul. It has survived for centuries, inspiring some of the greatest minds of all time, what would we not give for unlimited knowledge and power? It has been humanity's preoccupation since we climbed down from the trees. But would we give up our souls? Perhaps we already have—since spirituality is no longer taken very seriously by western civilization. For science and technology are now the reigning force of the day. Materialism, security, status and pleasure dominate most modern thought.

SOLARIS

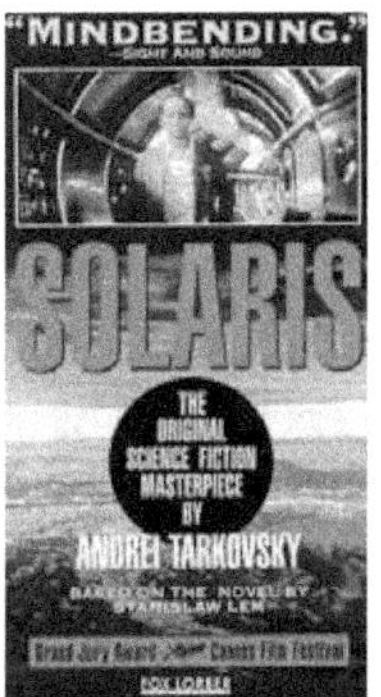

Director: Andrei Tarkovsky
Producer: Mosfilm Productions
Screenplay: Andrei Tarkovsky & Friedrich Gorenstein
From the novel by Stanislaw Lem
1972 Color/B & W
Russian with English subtitles

Solaris is a movie about self-discovery, relationships, and confronting one's own personal demons. It is also about truth and identity and self-actualization. Lem's cerebral science-fiction, along with Tarkovsky's visionary directing, result in a metaphysical movie with spiritual overtones.

In the future, a Soviet research team is in an orbiting space station above the alien world Solaris. The planet is covered almost entirely by ocean, an anomalous and complex ocean. The scientific study is far from routine. For the mysterious ocean seems to be sentient, perhaps even an alien intelligence.

And now, bizarre phenomena are occurring aboard the station. The official line is that members of the expedition are suffering from hallucinations. A specialist is called in, Kris Kelvin (Donatas Banionis), a psychologist who will not only investigate, but also determine the fate of the Solaris mission. For if the conditions are too dangerous, the project will be cancelled and the crew recalled.

Kelvin arrives at Solaris after a sixteen-month journey through space. He quickly discovers the odd behavior of the three-man crew. One had committed suicide just days before Kelvin arrived. The others are hiding something and seem somewhat paranoid. Something strange is definitely affecting the crew, and Kelvin soon realizes that there are others aboard. Aliens? But the crew seems to accept them with an embarrassed nonchalance.

The truth suddenly manifests during the night. Kelvin's long-dead wife, Hari, suddenly materializes at his bedside. She acts normal, like nothing is wrong, like she never died. Kelvin places her in a small rocket and blasts her into space. So much for that problem, or so he thinks. As he tries to understand what is happening, the crew finally break their silence. These manifestations always occur during the night, lingering on into the day—becoming stronger the more their presence is reinforced by interaction.

The scientists theorize that the ocean itself is an intelligent form of life, that it is trying to communicate, that it has the psychic power to reach into their subconscious during dreams. All the hidden fears, repressed desires, unspeakable feelings, and guilty consciences take shape and come to life—literally. Solaris naturally assumes that what we feel strongest about is what we care most about. The way to communicate with these alien earthlings is to tap into their passions and longings—the truth buried deep inside their psyches and souls. But what did the oceanic intelligence discover?—a dead wife for whom the ship's psychologist is consumed with guilt (because Kelvin drove her to suicide); a small dwarf who the astrobiologist keeps hidden in his lab; a little girl who the physiologist abandoned along with the rest of his family.

As the "visitors" interact, they become more familiar, more human. Kelvin even begins falling in love with his duplicate wife (the planet keeps making more). The crew realize it will all end badly unless they can communicate in some way other than through their dreams. They send a waking brain-wave encephalogram of Kelvin through an x-ray beam down into the ocean. It works! The duplicate visitors vanish. Instead, islands begin forming out of the ocean.

As the movie nears its end, a decision must be made. The others decide to remain, but Kelvin is considering returning to earth. After all, his reason for being sent has been resolved. The emergency is over. Normal research protocol can resume.

In Tarkovsky's interpretation of the Lem novel, he adds his own creative vision. The cinematic climax is a powerful revelation of the premise of Lem's book. But it is an ending which Lem failed to "materialize."

In Tarkovsky's ending, Kelvin is shown, once again, walking around the little lake near his father's home. This had been the opening scene before Kelvin left for Solaris. The viewer assumes that Kelvin has returned to earth and gone back home to see his father, to have that long-awaited talk for which they never seemed to have time. Before Kelvin had left earth, it was tacitly assumed they might never see each other again. The journey was sixteen months long—one way. Kelvin's dad was old, possibly had a medical condition.

Obviously the trip to Solaris had not been in vain, at least not for this psychologist. For he has returned with a new appreciation for all the psychic energy we keep stored in the frustration, resentments, hidden desires, and unacceptable truths. Solaris has shown him that these subconscious feelings are at the very core of his being. An alien intelligence had made the assumption that this inner world is what we are about—because it is what we feel and care most deeply about. Confirmation of this view comes from Kelvin's wife, Hari, as she becomes wiser and more human. In speaking of the duplicates, and therefore of herself, she says: "They are your conscience . . . They are yourselves!"

Deeply profound. And this is where Stanislaw Lem leaves his assessment of the crew's condition and their "relationship" with Solaris. However, Tarkovsky, in his visionary ending, cannot resist going one step further.

Everything seems normal as Kelvin walks up to the house. He has returned from outer space and is ready to explore the inner space of his relationship with his father. However, as Kelvin steps up to the cabin window, the audience realizes something is amiss. Water is dripping and puddling on the table and books. The dampness can almost be felt. The mustiness can almost be smelt.

As Kelvin looks in the window he sees his father walking about doing chores. Water is trickling down the window pane as though it has just rained. It is like a tropical rain forest. Water is dripping from the ceiling—inside the room, onto his father's back. Kelvin is nonplussed, for after all it is only to be expected. His father turns and notices Kelvin. He opens the front door and walks out onto the porch. Kelvin approaches and drops to his knees, hugging his father's legs.

The audience watches from above, as the camera pulls back. From above, we see the porch, the home, the yard surrounding the house, then the trees and the pond, the farm and the dirt road. As the house shrinks on the screen—suddenly water, a shoreline. It is a tiny island surrounded by a vast ocean—an intelligent ocean. Kelvin never left! He is still on Solaris.

The image and realization sends chills up the spine. Kelvin has remained behind, not only to continue contact with this strange alien intelligence, but also to deal with the inner world that has bound up his psychic energy with his father. He had already dealt somewhat successfully with his wife, Hari. Now it is his father's turn. That his "real" father isn't there scarcely seems to matter. For what is important is how we interpret and are affected by others. By dealing with his inner demons, Kelvin, the psychologist, will become a better person, as well as help communicate with an alien intelligence—a "two-for-one" serving a noble, metaphysical goal.

Tarkovsky's idealistic interpretation goes one step further than Lem, for not only is the neglected inner world the true power of our lives. But even in the absence of the objective world, our inner world takes precedence. For how we interpret, are affected by, and respond to others, comprises the very essence of our humanity—and our soul.

MY DINNER WITH ANDRÉ

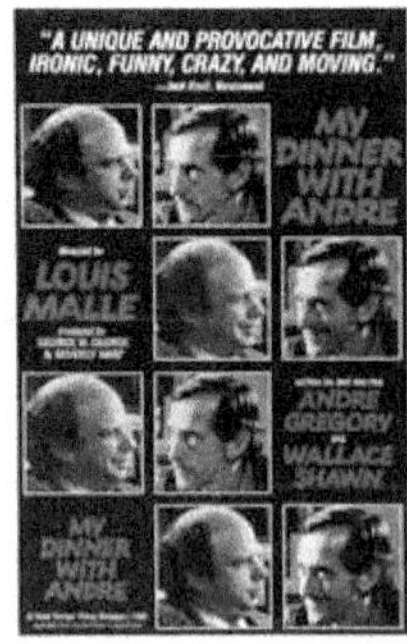

Director: Louis Malle
Producer: George W. George & Beverly Karp
Screenplay: André Gregory & Wallace Shawn
1981 Color

How committed are we to self-knowledge and the search for truth? How many of us truly wish to come face-to-face with reality? Would we be frightened? Would all our self-delusions come tumbling down around us? Would we have to sacrifice too much? Give up all we dearly love?

Director Louis Malle and writers André Gregory and Wallace Shawn create a daring movie about one man's quest for truth, and his attempt to share his insights with a former friend. What is bold about this independent film is that nearly the entire movie takes place around a dinner table. My Dinner with André is simply a conversation, nearly two hours long, about one man's adventurous quest to find himself.

The movie begins with Wallace Shawn (who plays himself) walking the streets of New York, running errands, reflecting over his life, and finally taking the subway to meet his estranged friend André Gregory (who also plays himself). Wally is dreading this encounter because of the rumors he has heard. André, once very successful as a theater director, suddenly gave up everything and dropped out of New York's artsy society. At one point he was in India and Tibet. At another, he was at Findhorn. At another, he was in charge of a Polish theatrical arts workshop in an ancient forest. Later, he was in the Sahara desert with a Japanese Buddhist priest. Most recently, he was in Montauk where he took part in a ritualistic, mock-burial alive.

Wally was talked into a meeting with André when a mutual friend found André sobbing uncontrollably on the street. He had just seen Ingmar Bergman's Autumn Sonata, and had been taken by Ingrid Bergman's line: "I could always live in my art, but never in my life." The profundity is portentous. Wally has trepidations of André disturbing his own simple life. He has problems of his own. Wally can't get his plays produced, can't find work as an actor. He is supported by his girlfriend who has to work as a waitress. And now, he is to meet André in an exclusive, posh restaurant.

André and Wally meet and are seated for dinner. Polite, but aloof waiters take their orders and serve intermittent courses throughout the two-hour dinner. What is surprising is that the conversation is intellectually stimulating and intriguing. We seem to be there, hanging on every word. Time passes quickly.

At first, Wally just listens and prods André with questions. André relates fantastic adventures with a new-age, counter-culture bent. Wally is noncommittal in his responses, but slowly his practical mind-set takes over. He argues from a pragmatic, realistic position. André argues as an inspired idealist. The two viewpoints clash, but always amicably and politely.

By the end of the movie we understand both points of view. We can take whatever metaphysical stance we please. But the lasting impression of My Dinner with André is that people are not facing reality. We have been brainwashed by both culture and society. We're like robots, responding automatically to the world around us. André may be a starry-eyed dreamer, an ivory-tower idealist who plunged off the deep end. But his passion to face reality, at all costs, strikes a deep chord and resonates in our soul. For it seems that as we age and graduate from the "school of hard knocks," the rest of us learn to give up, or give in. We compromise our ideals.

Strangely enough, Wally admits it was André himself who had given him his first break as a playwright. He had agreed to produce one of Wally's plays which became a success. Wally is indebted to this impractical idealist on a very practical level.

Now, at the end of the movie, the two find they have talked through the night. The restaurant is deserted. The waiters and busboys are covering the tables and preparing to close. When the bill arrives, André graciously insists on treating. Wally is taken aback by such generosity. His fear of a high-priced meal spontaneously combusts. His worries were for naught. He is once again indebted to his friend André, the dreamer.

Wally happily treats himself to a cab-ride home. On every street he sees a scene from his past. His entire life is passing before him through the windows of the taxi. It was a satisfying conversation, a liberating, dare one say, almost "enlightening" evening. He can't wait to get home and tell his girlfriend all about My Dinner with André.

PI

Faith in Chaos

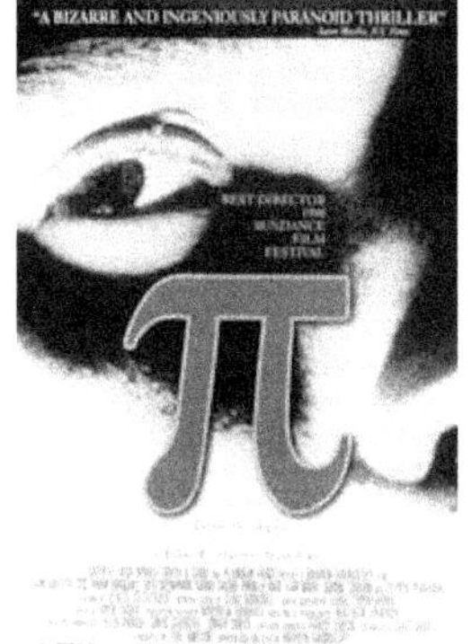

Producer: Eric Watson
Director: Darren Aronofsky
Screenplay: Darren Aronofsky, Eric Watson & Sean Gullette
1997 B & W

Pi is a "driven" movie about man's relentless search for truth. From the music score, with its repetitive urgency, to the undaunted research of Max (the protagonist played by Sean Gullette) and Euclid (his computer), the film pushes forward to its tragic finale.

Max is a genius mathematician who believes he is on the verge of discovering the theory of everything. He believes that mathematics is the language of the universe, and that its permutations pervade all existence—from the swirling cream in his coffee to the wispy curls of smoke from the puff of a cigarette. His second premise is that one can graph the mathematical expressions, finding patterns that can be deciphered to predict future manifestations.

Since mathematics underlies everything, patterns could even be discerned in the stock market. And therein lies the first complication: a group of powerful, corporate businessmen know what Max is onto—and they want in. They know that the research formula Max is about to uncover means wealth, power, and dominion over the earth.

The second complication comes from a group of Hassidic, cabalistic Jews. They believe that the impending discovery is actually the name of God: a 216 word numerological pattern that will reveal the secret of existence. Numbers, to them, are merely ciphers for words.

While working Max's program, Euclid is fried, but not before spitting out a message which Max cannot understand. He throws out the useless answer and disconsolately visits his mentor. This professor had initially worked on the program until a stroke forced him to prematurely retire. When Max reveals that Euclid's hodgepodge was around 200 numbers (or words), his mentor knows Max is close.

Meanwhile, the corporate group offers Max a powerful super-chip to revamp his computer. Max accepts and rediscovers the numbers. The corporate group is hot on his trail when he is rescued by the Hassidic Jews who also desperately want the answer. But Max, being the genius that he is, has memorized the 216 numbers. It is all in his head. Disclosing the information must now be voluntary.

Max returns to seek guidance from his mentor. But the professor has also rediscovered the numbers and has consequently died from a second stroke (lack of blood to the brain). Remember, Euclid (the computer) also had a blow-out of its brain when running the program had fried its circuits. And Max . . . Max, too, is having a breakdown. Or had he always been having a breakdown? Throughout the movie he has been taking pills and injections ostensibly for some physical condition. He becomes nervous and agitated, begins shaking, can't breathe.

But what if his condition isn't so much physical as mental? Paranoid schizophrenia manifests in much the same way as Max's behavior. He has half a dozen locks on his door. Checks through his peephole before emerging from his hole. Won't answer when someone knocks. Gets violently agitated when dealing with people. And what's more, and most importantly, schizophrenics see patterns in the world about them where normal people see chance and randomness.

Is this entire movie merely a sick psycho's delusion? Perhaps. Especially when considering the end. Frustrated and persecuted by both groups, despondent over his mentor's death, Max takes a power drill and sticks it in the side of his head.

As the movie ends, Max is at peace, apparently having survived his ordeal. He smiles at children playing in the park. The film fades out as he looks upward at the trees with all their millions of leaves. A pattern? Maybe.

And yet, there is another interpretation. Max was seeing underlying patterns in nature and society, because they do in fact exist. If there is a God or creative principle, if the Force or Universal Energy has a name. Perhaps it has 216 numbers. Perhaps Max has discovered the name of God. Perhaps it is, or was, all in his head. Perhaps the power drill was the only way to release the pressure of "everything" from his brain. Remember, his mentor had two strokes, the last had killed him. Even a mechanical computer blew its circuits because the program was too much. How could anything in creation presume to contain the Theory of Everything?

STALKER

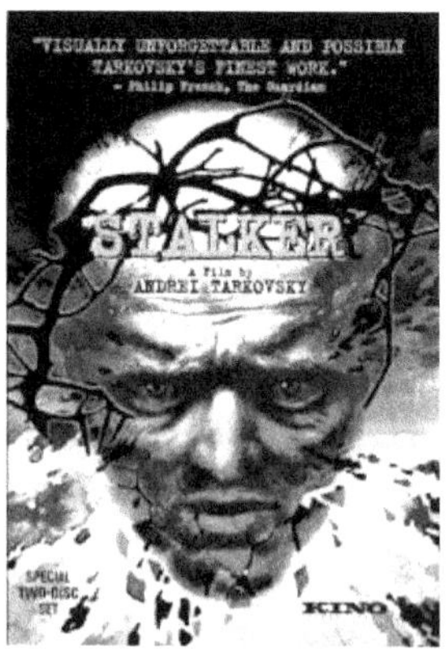

Director: Andrei Tarkovsky
Producer: Aleksandra Demidova
Screenplay: Arkady & Boris Strugatsky
From the novella "Roadside Picnic" by Arkady & Boris Strugatsky
1979 Color/B & W
Russian with English subtitles

What do we really want? Not, what do we think we want. Nor what others say we should want. Or what society believes we should want. But deep down, after all the sham is uncovered, what will truly make us happy? What do we believe in? What are our true desires? Who are we really?

In Stalker, Director Andrei Tarkovsky and writers Arkady and Boris Strugatsky examine these issues. It is a science-fiction film that borders on metaphysical mysticism. The premise is that an alleged meteorite crashed into a rural/industrial area causing strange phenomena and manifestations. Those who investigate do not return. Troops sent in disappear. Tanks, cannons, and armored vehicles sit idle, rusting, and covered with moss. The area is cordoned off with guards and barbed wire. It is illegal to enter "The Zone" until more can be understood.

The Zone exhibits the properties of a sentient intelligence. It has mood swings and an uncanny ability to see into the hearts of those who enter. Those with ulterior motives are rejected or punished. The Zone seems to admit only those who have lost hope and are desperate.

Nevertheless, certain individuals have developed the knack for guiding others safely into the Zone. They are "stalkers": criminals who are shot at, hunted down, and imprisoned. The only reason they still ply their trade is that the fee for entry is high, and, like it or not, they do bring back useful information for researchers and scientists.

What happens in the Zone? The laws of physics are topsy-turvy. Traps exist that kill or main. An area that is safe on one excursion is deadly on the next. Indeed, the landscape and conditions shift about so capriciously that one never returns the way one came. Only stalkers have proven reliable in leading people in and back out.

And so, why do people wish to enter the Zone? Besides curiosity, adventure, and the possibility of new discoveries and avenues of research—a rumor exists "that there's a place in the Zone where wishes come true." The authorities have been so baffled and thwarted by the Zone that they believe it may be true. Thus the need for guards and fences, the criminality of entering the Zone. For it's one thing to have your heart's desire if it is money or women or material objects. It is quite another, if a Hitler or Stalin enters the Zone and is granted world domination.

And now, back to the beginning plot of the movie. A stalker (Alexander Kaidanovsky) is engaged to lead two others into the Zone. A writer (Anatoly Solonitsyn) and a professor of physics (Nikolai Grinko) are the customers. Ostensibly, the Writer has lost his inspiration and hopes to find it. The Professor is looking for amazing discoveries, perhaps the Nobel Prize. But appearances aren't what they seem. It turns out that the Writer is searching for some sort of self-understanding. He admits:

> "Everything I told you before is a lie. I don't give a damn about inspiration. How would I know the right word for what I want? How would I know that actually I don't want what I want? Or that I actually don't want what I don't want? They are elusive things: the moment we name them, their meaning disappears, melts, dissolves like a jellyfish in the sun. My conscience wants vegetarianism to win over the world. And my subconscious is yearning for a piece of juicy meat.
> But what do I want?"

The structure of the movie is the slow movement through the Zone in search of the "Room." It is here that the seekers will receive their heart's content—that is, if they make it that far. Once again, many people die or are injured, most never return. Even stalkers are vulnerable to the Zone's deleterious effects.

The trek is painstakingly slow and methodical. The Stalker is guided by intuition as conditions change moment by moment. He uses nuts tied in bandages to scout and mark out the path. He throws them, and like dogs, the seekers must fetch and follow. They move slowly in each other's footsteps in a circuitous path that seems to lead them everywhere but to the Room. In the Zone, the most direct path isn't the shortest, although it could be the deadliest.

The seekers meander about fields and bogs, into run-down abandoned factories and murky tunnels. They wade through pools of water, climb up and down ladders. The atmosphere is that of a child's game. Serious playfulness with rules that change and are made up as they go along. Like children, they roll and crawl in the grass, lie listlessly in mud-puddles, and tumble about in sand dunes.

But it is a very dangerous game. For the side effects are real. Stalker's own daughter, "Monkey," is deformed as a result of his exposure to the Zone, although there is no detectable radiation. "They say she's got no legs."

And "Porcupine," Stalker's teacher, was also a victim. They say he was punished by the Zone. How? Why? Apparently Porcupine sent his own brother into the "Meat mincer" out of motivation for money. The brother died, and out of remorse, Porcupine visited the Room to get him back. When he returned to the outside world, he "got rich overnight. Fabulously rich. . . . A week later he hanged himself." Apparently the Room had searched his heart for his true desire, and found only greed. The brother didn't really matter. It was all about money.

Eventually the three wise men reach the Room. This isn't levity. The movie is replete with religious symbolism, both Christian and, of all things, Taoist. The Writer even dons a crown of thorns. But these symbols and allusions are not as important as the psychological theme.

And now for the Professor. It turns out that his real agenda is to destroy the Room. For "who knows what kind of wish someone might cherish." What if a madman or dictator reached the Room? It could be the end of humanity. It is too dangerous to allow the Room to exist.

It had been suspected for some time that the Zone was a result of alien visitation. The Room was possibly "a message to mankind . . . or a gift . . . to make us happy." But humans are too flawed. We are not worthy of such power: the ability to make any dream come true. It will all end in a nightmare unless it is quickly destroyed.

The Professor has constructed a portable nuclear bomb from components left by the first troop invasion, as well as from a trigger he himself has brought. The authorities don't want the Room destroyed. Despite the risk, they want it intact for further studies. But the Professor has taken it upon himself to carry out his own mission.

Stalker becomes frantic. He tries again and again to take the bomb from the Professor. But the Writer stands in his way, defending the Professor. After much argument and soul-searching, the Professor eventually dismantles the bomb and tosses the components away, leaving the Room to its own fate. But now nobody dares to even go into the Room. Nobody feels worthy to enter. They are afraid of their own desires, or perhaps of the Zone's retribution. And thus, all three return to the outer world, seemingly dejected and disillusioned.

Stalker is overcome by the effects of his soul-searching. The others don't believe in anything. The Writer maintains that "things like conscience, anguish, they are just inventions"—a sham to cover base desires such as Porcupine's greed. The Professor was ready to blow it all up because of his "desire" to keep humanity safe. Nobody has faith in our soul, or in what may lie beyond. For Stalker, the Zone and the Room represent man's last true hope for happiness. To destroy that last hope is what the scientist and the secular writer had almost accomplished.

The movie ends on a spiritual note. "Monkey," the mutant daughter, never says a word. She simply sits, staring intently at two glasses and a jar. They begin to slowly move across the table by the sheer force of her will. There is hope. The world has changed. Science and secular materialism no longer dominate, or have the last word. The Visitation has altered the course of human evolution. Supernatural phenomena and miracles are now taking shape. The scene closes with the exalting chorus of "Beethoven's Ninth."*

Stalker is a dream-like vision quest to find one's heart's desire. It is a soul-searching journey toward self-discovery: an in-depth look at values, beliefs, and psychological motivation. For the capricious and yet powerful labyrinth of the Zone, is that of one's own heart and mind. Tarkovsky and the Strugatsky brothers have created a visionary science-fiction film that explores, not outer space, but rather the interior of the human soul.

---

*The "Ninth Symphony" was composed when Beethoven was deaf. The music emanated from his heart and soul, but could not be perceived with his senses. The inner world took precedence over external reality. Beethoven could not "hear" the performance of his masterpiece. It emerged from and resonated only within the wellsprings of his soul.

SIDDHARTHA

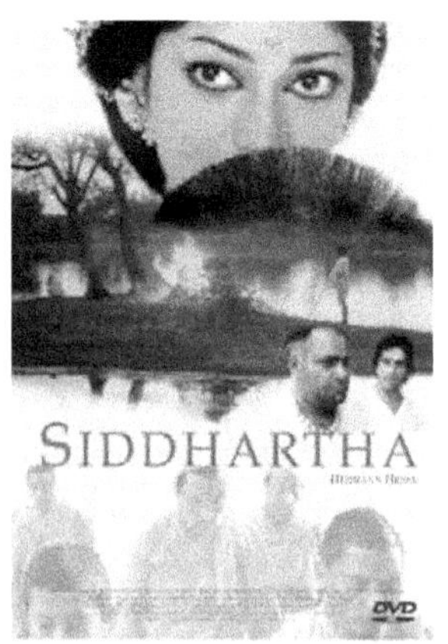

Director: Conrad Rooks
Producer: Conrad Rooks
Screenplay: Conrad Rooks
From the novel by Hermann Hesse
1972 Color

How many of us heathens haven't wondered what a deeply spiritual life would bring? We may admire and respect those fully dedicated to a mystical pursuit. But in the back of our minds it just doesn't seem right for us—at least not until we are so old that we are ready to greet the reaper. And yet, for some people there is nothing else but the pursuit of truth. Their entire lives are nothing other than the quest for enlightenment. To them, life itself is merely a distraction. For time is running out. They must achieve heaven or nirvana or bliss in this life cycle.

Siddhartha is the story of such a lifelong journey to know oneself, and thereby to know God or Buddha. Director/producer/writer Conrad Rooks adapts the popular novel by Nobel-prize winner Hermann Hesse. The story is loosely based upon the life of Buddha. However, Buddha is alive at the time, and Siddhartha even meets his namesake.

The movie begins as Siddhartha (Shashi Kapoor), a wealthy Brahmin's son, wishes to leave the comforts of his father's rich estate and become a Sadhu ascetic. His father is opposed, but stubborn Siddhartha wins out. He and his friend Govinda live for three years a half-starved, physically-punishing existence in the forest.

Eventually Siddhartha has had enough. He is no closer to enlightenment than he was at the start. He realizes that going from indulgence to deprivation is too extreme. He advocates the "middle way" of moderation.

Siddhartha leaves the ascetics, as well as Govinda, and meets Kamala, a lovely courtesan. She teaches him the way of the body and physical desire. Siddhartha's strict discipline makes him an excellent student. Kamala also introduces him to the world of commerce. One of her clients, Kamaswami, is a wealthy merchant who gives Siddhartha a job as his assistant. As usual, Siddhartha's mental focus makes him an excellent student. After years of hard work he excels to the level of an associate or partner. He has become master of the worldly ways and the ways of pleasure. He begins to sink into depravity: becomes abusive and petty, gambles and drinks, becomes self-indulgent and arrogant.

Suddenly, the true Siddhartha emerges. He is filled with disgust and self-loathing. What a waste he has become. He abandons his life, literally, and tries to drown himself in the river. But the holy river casts him out. It isn't his time.

Siddhartha then travels back to the ferryman, Vasudeva, who had once ferried him across the river for free. He becomes his apprentice, and is allowed to live in his hut.

Gradually, Siddhartha learns the wisdom of the river. It is connected from its source in the mountains down to its merging with the sea. It is at one with itself. It contains the beginning and the end. It is timeless. For at every moment it is present—everywhere at the same time. Its continuous flow is akin to a river of time. It is always changing. And yet it is always the same. One's entire life can be seen in its depths. For it is the source of all.

Eventually, after many years, Vasudeva decides to retire. Siddhartha may now take his place. He says good-bye and flows away down the river. Siddhartha is now the ferryman. He is like Charon, the Greek guide of the dead over the underworld river Styx. However, Siddhartha is the ferryman over the river of life.

Hermann Hesse's message, as well as that of the Buddha, is propounded by Siddhartha. One must stop the desire, even the desire for enlightenment, stop the unfulfilled searching, in order to find fulfillment in oneself. For desires and endless questing keep one always in the future. Whereas all one ever has is the present moment. As Buddha's main principle is that desire is the root of all suffering, so too does Siddhartha come to the same conclusion. After all, Siddhartha Gotama was, in reality, the historical Buddha Sakyamuni.

CHAPTER THREE

THE QUEST FOR SELF-REALIZATION

The journey begins and ends with oneself. The universe is whole in its seeming contradictions. The realization is an enlightening acceptance and affirmation.
It is "the way" that we all travel through life. Any dead ends and detours are a mere change of perspective.

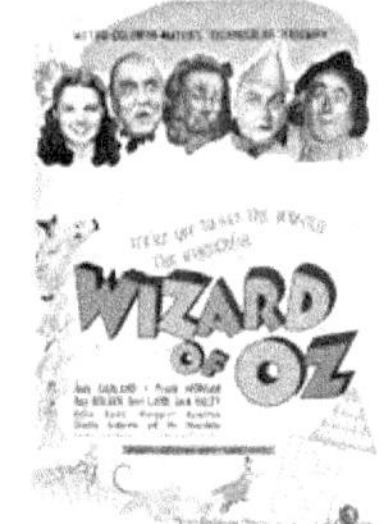

THE WIZARD OF OZ

Director: Victor Fleming
Producer: Mervyn LeRoy
Screenplay: Noel Langley, Florence Ryerson & Edgar Allan Woolf
From the book by L. Frank Baum, The Wonderful Wizard of Oz
1939 Color / B & W

A favorite of all, perhaps for its profound simplicity. Perhaps because it strikes a familiar chord deep within our psyche. The mythical, archetypal elements can be analyzed till the cows come home. But will Dorothy be with them? Of course, for it was all just a delirious dream.

What is the journey to Oz but a thinly-veiled quest for the Holy Grail?—the search for the sacred element that will enlighten man's soul. The quest for a brain, a heart, a home, and courage is the same as the quest for knowledge, love, belonging, and inner strength.

Dorothy doesn't know it yet, because she must experience it for herself through the school of hard knocks. But by the end of the film Dorothy realizes that every element of her amazing journey actually has its counterpart in real life. The Scarecrow, the Tin Man, and the Cowardly Lion are the zany farmhands. The Wizard is the itinerant Professor Marvel. The Wicked Witch is the mean neighbor who wants to kill Toto.

Dorothy's fantastic excursion to Oz was simply the mythical substrate of her everyday life on the farm. To find her soul, her heart's desire, she need look no further than her own backyard. "Because if it isn't there, I never really lost it to begin with." The grass is always greener on the other side—somewhere over the rainbow. But L. Frank Baum would beg to differ. Dorothy's running away from home was actually a running away from herself. But it was a flight necessary to truly find herself once again at home. Because all true quests ultimately return to the source.

The movie climaxes when the Wizard is defrocked by Toto. The Great Oz is merely a charlatan—"the man behind the curtain"—pulling levers and turning wheels to create an illusion. But it is all for show. The Wizard is, once again, the playful, light-hearted trickster. And yet he is also the holy fool. For he realizes that our reality is contingent upon our faith and belief. And so, the Tin Man is given a testimonial for his kindness, and a keepsake watch in the shape of a heart for his love and compassion in saving Dorothy. The Cowardly Lion is awarded a Triple Cross for bravery in battling wicked witches. And the Scarecrow is presented with a scroll, a degree from the University of Oz?—and suddenly he is a "Wiz" at everything intellectual.

The Wizard of Oz knows that faith and belief are the most powerful forces in life. As we believe and try, so will we eventually overcome all obstacles. Nothing can stand in the way if we abolish self-doubt—especially if it is, after all, only a dream.

And what about Dorothy? "Yes, how about Dorothy?" What did she learn? She learned, "There's no place like home." As the Wizard accidentally leaves her behind, the Good Witch Glinda tells her that she always had the power to return. All she had to do was to believe fully that she could.

And so Dorothy returns home to find all the familiar faces, the "usual suspects," the mythical-archetypal elements shadowing everyday life. The magic resides everywhere. The Land of Oz over the rainbow is actually the mythological substrate—the aboriginal "Dreamtime" underlying modern life.

"Somewhere over the rainbow . . .
Skies are blue . . .

And the dreams that you dare to dream . . .
Really do come true."

ALICE'S ADVENTURES IN WONDERLAND

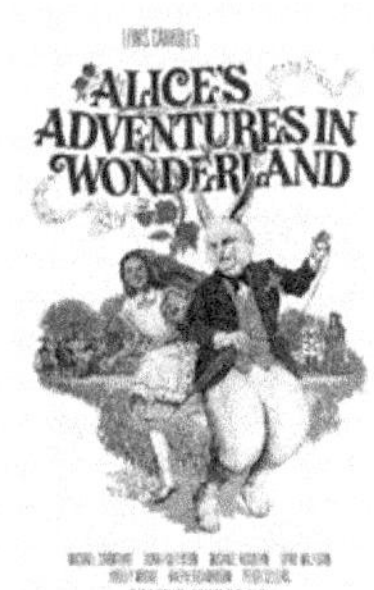

Director: William Sterling
Producer: Derek Horne
Screenplay: William Sterling
From the novel by Lewis Carroll
1972 Color

While there are a profusion of films about Alice's Adventures, my favorite is the British version of 1972. William Sterling directs Lewis Carroll's tale with Fiona Fullerton starring as Alice.

For all the myriad interpretations and studies of Alice in Wonderland, the common chord is a thinly-veiled parody of modern life. Whether the satire is social, political, religious, or philosophical, the theme is a biting, and yet lighthearted spoof of Victorian life and western civilization. Carroll disguises his commentaries from the innocence of a child's perspective, using animals and farcical humans as actors in his adventure. A dream-structure is employed to provide fantastical transpositions and transformations. A deck of live playing-cards create the atmosphere and court-venue for the story.

The movie begins with: "A boat, beneath a sunny sky, lingering onward dreamily in an evening of July."[1] Lewis Carroll is on an outing with the three little Liddell sisters of whom Alice is one. A story is begun in real life, and is finished by Alice falling asleep and dreaming its conclusion.

Alice chases a talking White Rabbit down a rabbit hole to an underground world. She shrinks and grows in size much to everyone's amazement and consternation. She moves from scenario to scenario unsure of her identity. She is mistaken for a maid, is questioned by a large Caterpillar. "Who are you?" Alice is at a loss. "I can't explain myself . . . because I'm not myself, you see."

Alice meets the Duchess and her pepper-cook, as well as a baby who mutates into a wriggling pig. She encounters the Cheshire Cat who appears and vanishes always beginning and ending with a smile. She then finds her way to Tweedledee and Tweedledum who agree to have a battle over a toy rattle. Afterward, Alice is <u>un</u>invited to a mad tea party hosted by the March Hare, the Mad Hatter and the Dormouse, who are all as crazy as most grown-ups.

Alice finally discovers the beautiful, little garden she has been trying to enter since the beginning of her adventure. It is a royal garden inhabited by a kingdom of playing cards. The entire deck parades about, showing deference to the King and Queen of Hearts. The royal hierarchy pervades all aspects of Wonderland. They provide the structure for all of Alice's adventures. But, in the final analysis, it is only a game.

Alice plays croquet with royalty using live flamingos and hedgehogs. She then meets the Gryphon, a mythological creature whose trademark line is, "It's just his fancy." For people imagine and exaggerate all their problems and sorrows. Alice, the Gryphon, and the Mock Turtle then sing and dance the Lobster Quadrille with wild abandon.

At a sham trial held by the King and Queen of Hearts, Alice grows to gargantuan proportions. She is told to leave the courtroom, but she won't. She is no longer intimidated. "You're nothing but a pack of cards!" The cards fly up into her face, and Alice awakens with leaves and petals falling on her face.

It's time to go home. It's getting late. The boating party drifts back along the beautiful river. Alice has been to Wonderland, and she is now quickly growing up, ready to marvel at the adult world with childish bewilderment. "From now I'll be the me I never knew."

Director William Sterling and writer Lewis Carroll have created a beautiful story which is one of the world's enduring classics. <u>Alice's Adventures in Wonderland</u> is more than just a children's story. For it lives in the hearts and minds of all who have grown into adulthood. It is cherished by millions, translated into most foreign languages for children throughout the world to enjoy.

What message does it hold? The various interpretations are endless. But for many it embodies the wonder and imagination of childhood. It also portends the serious world of grown-ups, which all children are anxious to enter, but which is really just another game. In a playful and lighthearted manner, <u>Alice's Adventures in Wonderland</u> is a spoof on adult life—warning children that adulthood shouldn't be idealized too seriously. For it is in the wonder and innocence of childhood happiness that true paradise lies.

1. Lewis Carroll, Alice in Wonderland: and Through the Looking-Glass (Kingsport: Grosset & Dunlap, Publishers, 1978), p. 307.

KUNGFU

Director: Jerry Thorpe
Producer: Jerry Thorpe
Screenplay: Ed Spielman & Howard Friedlander
1972 Color

Why is it spirituality is often associated with physical weakness? Is it because, "the meek shall inherit the earth?" Is it because those who are spiritual are usually told to abhor violence? (This obviously excludes religious terrorists along with the shameful history of religious warfare.) Is it because of the classic image of a half-starved Indian ascetic who wouldn't, or couldn't, harm a fly? Or of heavily robed monks and priests who are cloistered in their churches and monasteries without the benefit of making a living through physical labor outdoors? Perhaps it is because of the non-violent protests of Gandhi or of Martin Luther King? Or perhaps it is the image of a Buddhist monk immolating himself with burning gasoline out of protest to the Vietnam war? Or is it the stories of Tibetan Buddhist monks being killed by the thousands as Chinese communists bombarded their monasteries and then executed all who survived?

In any case, the prejudice remains: the nice guy always finishes last. Ruthlessness and barbarism seem to be the province of the immoral and evil. Consequently, the religious and spiritual appear physically inept, or, at the very least, seriously disadvantaged.

Director Jerry Thorpe and writers Ed Spielman and Howard Friedlander give us another vision. From out of the enchanted culture of China, and the not-too-distant American West, comes the movie Kung Fu (the pilot for the popular television series). The monks and priests of the Shaolin temple studied the martial arts in order to attain physical and mental discipline and perfection. Their way of life was spiritual, and yet they were strong in both body and mind.

The fantasy appeals to all who have "turned the other cheek." Why can't the good be powerful, held in respect and awe? Kung Fu shows the way to be both good and "bad," to fight only in defense of oneself or others. But when one does, to really kick ass!

The movie begins showing Kwai Chang Caine (David Carradine) hiking up and down the sand dunes of the American desert. When he arrives in town, the barkeeper laughs in disbelief at his claim to have crossed the desert on foot. However, a fight breaks out, and Caine disarms his opponent in a dazzling display of fighting prowess, and without even harming him. The crowd become believers.

The plot of the movie is unimportant. What is intriguing are the continual flashbacks to Caine's past. Scenes of monastic life are interspersed with life in the American West during the mid-nineteenth century. From China, we see the trials and ordeals of growing up in the Shaolin monastery. Young Caine (Radames Pera) must undergo severe discipline and training, as well as good, old-fashioned, hard work. But he is also surrounded by loving kindness, a brotherhood that would sacrifice anything for its members.

The movie shows how young Caine was first admitted to the order. After days of waiting outside the gate, sometimes in pouring rain, he passes test after test of patience, endurance, simple manners and politeness. However, only full-blooded Chinese have ever been accepted into the Shaolin, and Caine is half-American. But as the head priest, Master Kan, explains with a smile: "There is a first for everything."

Respect and dignity, morals and ethics are instilled in Caine. He advances in all aspects of his studies as he grows to adulthood. He excels in the physical disciplines till it is "time for him to leave." Caine, the adult, is ready for the life of a wandering Shaolin priest. But he must be initiated, fully, by lifting a cauldron of burning coals with the insignia of the dragon and tiger on its sides. The scarred designs will be seared into the flesh of his bare arms as Caine places the cauldron on a stone pedestal. A spring mechanism opens the door to the outer world. Caine is released, branded with the mark of spirituality and respect.

Director Jerry Thorpe and writers Ed Spielman and Howard Friedlander have succeeded in portraying a mysterious, esoteric sect. The Shaolin are a matter of historical fact. The monastery, which had been burnt to the ground, has recently been restored. It is now a tourist attraction and propaganda tool for the Chinese communists.

Kung Fu (the pilot movie), as well as the popular television series which it spawned, provided millions of Americans with a unique vision of oriental spirituality. One can be strong and disciplined, and yet still be humble and spiritual. For the strength resides within, not in the physical exterior.

ALICE THROUGH THE LOOKING GLASS

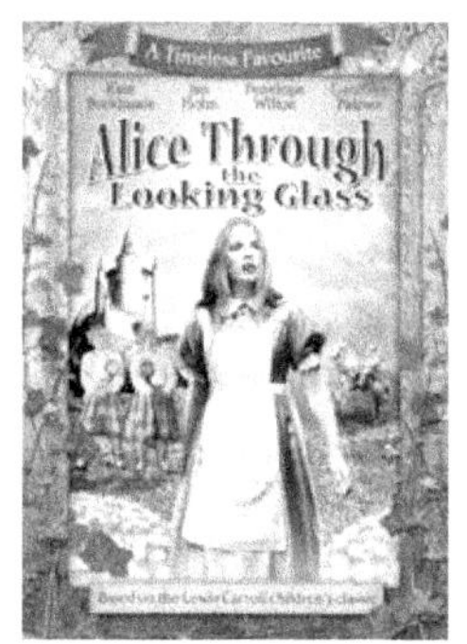

Director: John Henderson
Producer: Simon Johnson & Trevor Eve
Screenplay: Nick Vivian
From the novel by Lewis Carroll
1997 Color

Alice has grown to adulthood, becoming a woman and mother. While this departs from Lewis Carroll's original novel, it nevertheless remains faithful as a sequel to Alice's Adventures in Wonderland. So much of "Wonderland" was filled with growing in size and joining the adult world. Now Alice has done so, but as she passes "Through the Looking Glass" she is, once again, only "seven and a half, exactly." Although a mother to a little daughter, she herself is still a child at heart. Lewis Carroll would have been proud.

In Alice Through the Looking Glass, director John Henderson and writer Nick Vivian create the most authentic version of Lewis Carroll's classic fairy tale. While the action may be slow to some critics, a faithful rendition of a novel is apt to be slow-moving in parts. Hollywood attention-span is incompatible with most classic literature. In any case, the cinematography is beautiful.

The movie begins with the adult Alice (Kate Beckinsale) transforming into the spirit of a seven-and-one-half-year-old girl. She passes Through the Looking Glass and discovers another strange world akin to Wonderland. The Red Queen introduces Alice to Looking Glass World:

"It's marked out just like a large chessboard!" exclaims Alice.
"It's a great huge game of chess that's being played—all over
the world.

Oh, how I wish I was one of the players."

Alice's wish is granted. She is allowed to play, but only as a beginning white pawn—the least powerful and most vulnerable of all the chess pieces. The Red Queen instructs Alice about her position on the board as well as her forward movement through to the eighth square. Before departing she warns Alice ominously, "And remember who you are."

And so one senses, from the start, that identity and one's place in the world are major themes in the movie. So too, is the game-structure upon which the film and action unfold. For movement of characters is linked to their roles as chess pieces. The Red and White Queens are fast-forwarded as they move from scene to scene (since the queens can move the farthest in any direction on the board). Alice suddenly appears in a leaping railway carriage as she proceeds quickly two squares on her first move. The two opposing knights must fight as Alice's position on square seven is in jeopardy. And finally, Alice becomes a queen when she is crowned on reaching the eighth square.

Back on square four, Alice meets the Tweedle brothers and they come upon the sleeping Red King. If one dismisses Lewis Carroll as mere childish fantasy, take a gander at this metaphysical dialogue:

"He's dreaming now. What you think he's dreaming about?"
asks Tweedledee.

"Well, nobody can guess that," says Alice.

"Why, about you! If he left off dreaming about you, where do
you suppose you'd be?"

"Where I am now, of course," says Alice.

" . . . Not you! You'd be nowhere. Why, you're only a sort of
thing in his dream!"

"If that there King was to wake up now, you'd disappear . . ." adds Tweedledum.

"If I'm just a sort of thing in his dream, what does that make you, I should like to know?" challenges Alice.

"Ditto," says Tweedledum,

"Ditto, ditto!" cries Tweedledee.

"Hush! You'll be waking him if you make so much noise," scolds Alice.

"Well, it's no use you talking about waking him when you're only one of the things in his dream," says Tweedledum. "You know very well that you're not real."

"I am real," objects Alice, and begins to cry.

"I am real!" mocks Tweedledee. "You won't make yourself a bit realer by crying. There's nothing to cry about."

"But if I wasn't real, I wouldn't be able to cry," objects Alice.

"I don't suppose you hope those are real tears," remarks Tweedledum.

This is no children's fairy tale. Rather, it is an epistemological and ontological exchange over the nature of reality. Are we merely passing thoughts in the mind of God? Do we really exist? Or is life just a dream? And, if so, whose dream?

The game continues. Alice now lands on square five where she meets the White Queen who transforms into an old sheep in a curio shop. Alice is unable to look at the merchandise directly, for "Things flow about so, here." Objects of every kind seem to be all around, but when she tries focusing, they move out of the corner of her vision. "It's quite provoking." Could this be a prelude to Heisenberg's Principle of Uncertainty? In quantum physics, reality can't be pinned down. In order to examine subatomic particles you must bombard them with electrons or other subatomic particles. This bombardment necessarily alters their movement, as well as their state of energy. Trying to know reality, uncontaminated, as it is right now, is impossible. The problem is referred to as the "observer phenomenon." The observer interacts with and alters the observed. Similarly, as Alice reaches for the egg she purchased in the curio shop: "Oh, the egg seems to get further away, the more I walk towards it." For one can only arrive at an approximation of reality. The closer one tries to get, the more it is transformed.

Alice's pursuit of the egg lands her on square six with Humpty Dumpty. Humpty fancies himself an expert linguist, and a logician, to boot. His arguments may seem like meaningless rhetoric, but mere sophistry they are not. Indeed, they are sophisticated, and yet humorous discourses upon linguistics and semantics. In Lewis Carroll's novel, Humpty maintains: "When I use a word, it means just what I choose it to mean—neither more nor less."[1] Likewise, Alice's encounter with the White Knight on square seven follows up the semantic argument:

"The name of the tale is called 'Haddock's Eyes,'" says the White Knight.

"Oh, that's the name of the tale, is it?" remarks Alice.

"No, that's something quite different. That's what the name of the tale is called. The name really is 'The Aged Aged Man.'"

"Oh, so I ought to have said 'That's what the tale is called'?" Alice corrected herself.

"No, you oughtn't: that's quite another thing! The tale is called 'Ways and Means': but that's only what the tale is called, see?"

"Well, then what is the tale, then?" asks Alice, completely bewildered.

"I'm coming to that," says the Knight. "The tale really is 'A-sitting On A Gate' …"

---

1 Lewis Carroll, Through the Looking-Glass: and What Alice Found There (New York: Random House, Inc., 1946), p. 94.

The logic is impeccable. Ask some child or even some grown-up to follow its twists and turns. For most, the words go in one ear and out the other. Words are simply names for describing a common reality. But the Gnat informs Alice that "In the woods over there, they have no names." Perhaps that is the reason for the Red Queen's warning: "Remember who you are."

Alice remembers who she is and eventually does become a White Queen (after failing some grueling and ridiculous tests). After being crowned, there is a dinner banquet which turns into pandemonium. Alice awakens to find herself back in the "real" world—or should one just say the "normal" world? For what is reality? And "Which Dreamed it?" (which is the title of the last chapter of the book). Lewis Carroll answers these questions in the closing poem which also closes the movie with fade out:

In a Wonderland they lie
Dreaming as the days go by,
Dreaming as the summers die:

Ever drifting down the stream—
Lingering in the golden gleam—
Life, what is it but a dream?

WALKABOUT

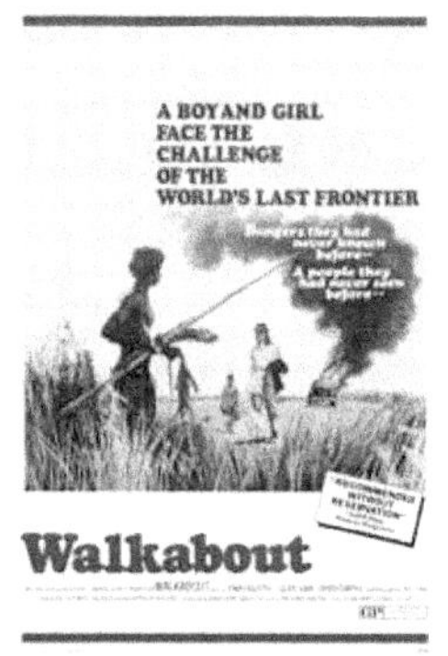

Director: Nicolas Roeg
Producer: Si Litvinoff & Max L. Raab
Screenplay: Edward Bond
From the novel by James Vance Marshall
1971 Color

"Walkabout" is the rite of passage of an Australian aborigine adolescent. When he turns sixteen, the aborigine male must fend for himself in the harsh Australian Outback. This six-month ordeal, if it is survived, will transform him into a man. It is similar to the Native American vision quest—a rite of initiation.

Walkabout, the movie, is about such a quest for manhood. But it is also the walkabout of two English children: a schoolgirl (Jenny Agutter) on the verge of becoming a woman, and her brother, a small boy (Lucien John). Director Nicolas Roeg creates a moving and beautiful drama of what happens when all three combine. The clashing of cultures. The struggle for survival. The oneness of all nature which is, nevertheless, in brutal conflict.

The movie begins in a modern city in Australia. The father, a geologist, drives his two children into the Outback for a picnic. Depressed and unbalanced, he shoots at them, misses, and the children run off and hide. He then pours gasoline over the car, sets it ablaze, and then shoots himself with the pistol.

There is now no quick way home. The children must walk back to civilization on their own. With what little food and drink the girl is able to salvage from the aborted picnic, the two set off into the Outback. The sun, the heat, the eventual lack of food and water take their toll. The children seem doomed to die beneath the shelter of a shadeless tree at a dried-up water hole.

All seems hopeless when, literally out-of-the-blue, a figure darts about the sandy hillside. It is an aborigine boy (David Gumpilil) hunting lizards on his walkabout. The aborigine soon realizes the helplessness of the children. They can scarcely communicate, but through pantomime he understands that they need water. His native aboriginal skills quickly fill their need. His bushcraft and wilderness wisdom ensures their survival. He hunts and cooks for them while leading them toward civilization. The trek takes days, during which they become friends, playing and working toward their goal.

Eventually, the aborigine brings them to the outskirts of civilization. They take overnight refuge in an old, abandoned farmhouse. Close by he shows the boy a paved highway. One more day traveling will bring them to a town.

This is the last chance for the aborigine who desires the young girl to be his wife. An all-night, dance ritual fails to woo her to his side. She is frightened and remains inside the farmhouse with her brother. In the morning they find him hanging from a tree. His rejection had been devastating. The one who saved two, now dangles dead.

The children return to the civilized world. The movie ends with a glimpse into the future. The girl, now a young woman in her twenties, is in the same apartment building in which she lived as a child. But now she is married. Her husband returns home from work while she is preparing dinner. He babbles about office politics as a dreamy look enters her eyes.

She sees herself in the Outback with her little brother and the aborigine. They are happy, at one with nature, swimming naked in a beautiful, oasis pool. The earthly paradise of the primitive world—simple, idyllic. She wonders, in her fantasy, how life might have been had she remained.

Director Nicolas Roeg and writer James Vance Marshall create a beautiful tale of the conflicting urges within man. Fast-paced society with all its complexities and drawbacks or the uncomplicated primitive world with natural instincts and simple needs. Technology and the global merging of cultures drive us one way. Embracing nature and cultural preservation lead us back to our ancestral roots. It seems all but certain which will prevail. Perhaps primitivism will only survive in the dreams and fantasies of a few. Perhaps religion and art can preserve its spirit. Or perhaps only in the mythological Dreamtime of the Aborigines will the natural spirit live on.

CHAPTER FOUR

SELF-CONSCIOUS PATTERNS OF MEANING

The quest for meaning comes full circle, returning to the source. Its path describes an intricate network of patterns. The meaning overlaps and refers back to itself. It is a maze, a mirror of self-reflection. The labyrinthine movements begin to make sense. The solution, the key, Ariadne's thread. The puzzle is nearly solved. The meaning of life is the snake eating its own "tale."

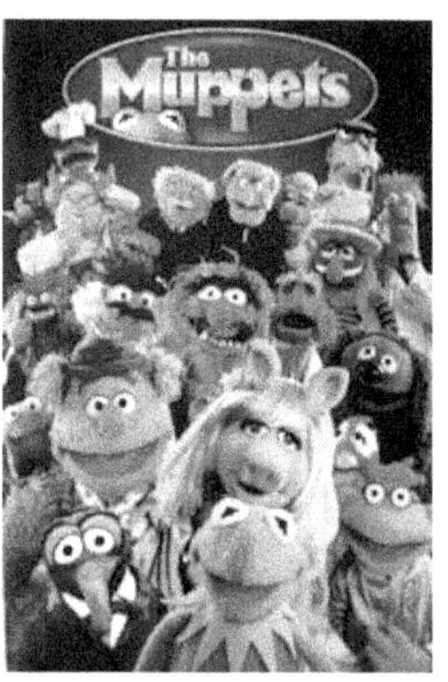

THE MUPPET MOVIE

Producer: Jim Henson
Director: James Frawley
Screenplay: Jerry Juhl & Jack Burns
1979 Color

While a joke to most people, The Muppet Movie is a profound and yet humorous and lighthearted film. Its dual nature plays upon the trickster theme of the holy fool. We can laugh at the juvenile antics, but we are really laughing at ourselves. The simplistic nature of the cartoon is really a thinly-disguised parody of our own simple lives.

The film is about Kermit's journey from his swamp-home to Hollywood. It's about "how the muppets really got started." They are following their dream, auditioning for a movie that will make them into stars. And yet the scenes and events in their quest for fame constitute the movie itself. Their journey to Hollywood is actually the theme of The Muppet Movie.

When Kermit and Fozzie Bear meet Doctor Teeth and The Electric Mayhem, an awareness of the "audience" causes a self-conscious change in the plot. Kermit has them read the screenplay of The Muppet Movie so that they can catch up with the action while he and Fozzie catch up on their sleep. What develops thematically is a self-referential movie—a Mobius film strip that turns in on itself, inverts, and returns to the infinite beginning.

While stranded in the desert, Kermit and his cohorts are rescued by The Electric Mayhem.

"How did you ever find us?" asks Kermit in amazement.

Doctor Teeth holds up the script of The Muppet Movie.

"Oh, easy, we just read the screenplay you left us. 'Exterior. Desert. Night.'
We knew right where you were."

The Muppets make it to Hollywood and are hired to produce their own movie—The Muppet Movie. Kermit directs as the others re-create the set. They have become the stars of their own adventures. But something has to give.

As the action accelerates, and the characters replay their scenes; the sets, props, and equipment begin to implode and explode. The whole scene collapses as the end nears the beginning. A rainbow magically shines through the broken roof and illuminates the Muppets on stage. It is "The End." But not yet the end of The Muppet Movie.

As the film nears its conclusion all the characters are in on the joke. They are seated in the audience watching the premiere of The Muppet Movie. But this audience scene, itself, is also part of The Muppet Movie. How can this be? They will be watching themselves on the screen watching themselves on the screen in an infinite regress! It is maddening. The only way out of the infinite loop is for something drastic to happen.

Jack "the job" (alias "Sweetums"), an eight foot tall shaggy monster has been running late throughout the journey to Hollywood. He finally catches up with his fellow Muppets and bursts through the movie screen they are watching.

"Oh, I just knew I'd catch up with you guys!" he screams with laughter, hoping he's not too late. On the contrary, although the movie is ending, he is, and will always be, exactly on cue.

What the structure of the film seems to be implying, by this circular and reflective theme, is that life is actually a movie. Our everyday life is the theme for the drama of our existence. We are all the stars, the heroes and heroines of an Academy Award-winning movie. How we act and interact is there for all to see. And it has been recorded for all time.

In Hinduism this witness of events is known as the Akashic Record. In after-life and near-death experiences many say their "life passed before their eyes." Wouldn't it be a lark if, at the moment of death, we were all treated to an encore presentation of The Muppet Movie? So much for a mere children's cartoon.

Or, as Kermit sings at the film's finale:

"Life's like a movie,
Write your own ending . . .
Keep believing,
Keep pretending . . ."

THE PURPLE ROSE OF CAIRO

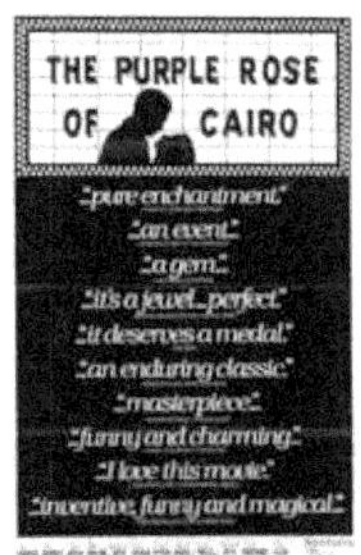

Director: Woody Allen
Producer: Robert Greenhut
Screenplay:Woody Allen
1984 Color

The Purple Rose of Cairo is Woody Allen's ingenious masterpiece about the dichotomy between idealism and real, practical life. Cecelia (Mia Farrow) is the starry-eyed dreamer who loves movies and fantasies. Fed up with her boring, depressing lifestyle, she takes refuge in cinema. Her marriage is a failure. She is used and abused by her unfaithful leech of a husband. And to top it all, she is fired from her job during the height of the Depression.

Cecelia visits the cinema night after night, watching her favorite movie over and over, when suddenly she is noticed by one of the characters on screen. The movie-reel pauses as the character talks to Cecelia from the screen. He is attracted to her, wants to know more about her and the "outside" world. He steps out of the screen and into real life. The other characters on the screen are appalled. What are they supposed to do? The movie can't go on.

The audience is equally both shocked and amused. Many demand their money back. Others are curious how the problem will resolve.

Meanwhile, Cecelia shows the "character" around the town. Romance blossoms. Compared to her husband, Tom is ideal. And indeed, he is truly fictional. And therein lies the problem. The ideal world is by definition superior to mundane reality. But at least mundane reality is real. It is tangible. It can be grasped.

The impracticality of the ideal is evident when Tom and Cecelia must pay for their dinner. Tom tries to pay in phony stage money and Cecelia is broke. And so they are forced to skip out on the bill. But the ideal world also has its benefits. After a brawl with Cecelia's husband, Tom doesn't have a mark. In fact, every hair on his head is in place. He is perfect and unmarred. "I don't get hurt or bleed. . . . one of the advantages of being imaginary."

Cecelia has doubts as her heart is torn between practical reality and ivory-tower fantasies. And now another complication enters the scene. Movie theaters are having problems all over the country. Other "Toms" are trying to walk "off screen." The motion picture industry is paralyzed. In panic, the agent and producer send Gil Shepard, the real actor, to Cecelia's town. His task is to convince the original "walk-off" to return to the screen.

Cecelia and the "real" actor meet. He also begins wooing Cecelia, but with a different agenda. He merely wants her to reject Tom so that he will return to the screen and set the film back in motion. Moviedom will then be saved, as well as the real actor's career.

In the meantime, Tom, "the ideal character," entices Cecelia to enter his cinematic world of illusion. If he can't exist in the real world, then maybe Cecelia can exist in his. They enter the silver screen and have a whirlwind night on the town. But eventually, as do all films, the fairy-tale movie must end. Cecelia, like Cinderella, must return to the humdrum cinders of the real world.

As they step out of the screen they are confronted by Gil, the real actor. He demands that the ideal Tom return to the screen. He claims, disingenuously, that he too loves Cecelia. He wants her to leave her husband. He wants to take her back to Hollywood. Tom, the ideal, also wants Cecelia for himself. True love will conquer all, surmount any problem—real or fictional.

Cecelia is torn once again. The real actor or the ideal character? Most of the cast of characters on screen tell her to choose the real-life actor. That's the only practical solution: a real person with a real person in the real world. But do they just want Tom, the ideal, to return to the screen so that the movie can continue? One character, however, advises Cecelia to choose the ideal Tom. True love may never come your way again. It's ideal. Don't give it up for what's practical. "You're throwing away perfection."

Cecelia chooses. She wants the real actor. The disappointed ideal Tom returns reluctantly to the screen. All is well. Cecelia goes home and dumps her husband.

She returns to the theater only to find the real actor has already flown the coop. He simply used her to save his career. Practical reality has once again let her down.

The ideal world, in contrast, would have never let her down because, by its very definition, it is perfect and ideal. Cecelia's choice may have been wrong, but the tide is about to turn. Woody Allen ends his own Purple Rose of Cairo in a sentimental, and yet uplifting and even inspiring climax.

Cecelia, homeless as a bag-woman, carries her suitcase into the movie house—the only sanctuary that remains. The on-going film stars Fred Astaire and Ginger Rogers. Astaire is singing the famous song "Cheek to Cheek" to Ginger as he woos her on screen.

As Cecelia seats herself she is dejected and heartbroken. The emptiness shows on her face—the vacant expression, the dead eyes. But as she watches and listens as Astaire and Rogers sing and dance across the stage, a certain interest and curiosity brings a little glow to her eyes. The graceful, flowing movements of a dance couple moving as one brings delight and light into her eyes. It is a harmonious blending of athletic prowess and singing talent. It is wonderful. It is perfection. It is ideal. It is a real dream.

The lighting on Cecelia's face brightens. Her face is aglow. The dreams, the hopes, the ideals have returned. In the final, memorable scene, Cecelia's parted lips slightly smile.

"Heaven. . . . I'm in heaven. . . .
And my heart beats so that I can hardly speak. . . .
And it seems I find the happiness I seek . . .
When we're out together dancing cheek to cheek. . . ."

THE HYPOTHESIS OF THE STOLEN PAINTING

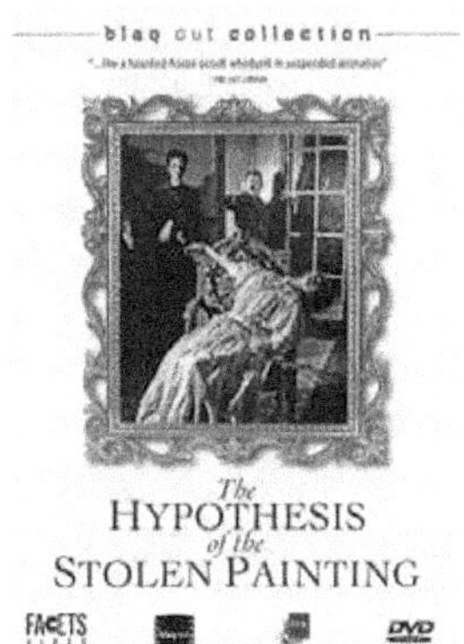

Director: Raul Ruiz
Producer: Nedjma Ouichene for
L' Institut National de L' Audiovisuel
Screenplay: Raul Ruiz & Pierre Klossowski
From the novel, Baphomet, by Pierre Klossowski
1978 B & W
French with English subtitles

In The Hypothesis of the Stolen Painting, Chilean director/writer Raul Ruiz creates an intricate, metaphysical film on par with the writings of Jorge Louis Borges. The movie is a detective story through the world of art, a jigsaw puzzle using seven different, but interlinked paintings of which one is missing.

The story and plot are ingenious. Paintings come to life in "tableaux vivants," or living artworks in which actors or models remain frozen in the static postures portrayed in the paintings. The camera moves from one artwork to another, following the narration of a rich art collector who has six of the seven paintings. His whole life revolves around the series. It is his singular obsession.

The movie begins with an unseen narrator introducing the mystery behind the artworks. The nineteenth century painter, Frédéric Tonnerre, caused a scandal with the exhibition of his series of seven paintings, a scandal which escalated to become an affair of state replete with police raids and a consequent cover-up. The mystery and question is, "Why?" Most of the canvases seem innocuous enough: diverse in style and subject matter, with no apparent common theme. Was it all because of the missing seventh painting? Or was it the interlinking of the pictures that was scandalous? Now that one is missing, has the chain been broken? Have they all been rendered harmless because the missing link has severed the meaning?

The narrator and camera follow the art collector who does most of the explaining. He begins analyzing the first medieval painting: a dark room in which two crusaders (Knights Templar) sit playing chess. All seems normal till the collector points out that there are two sources of light flooding the room from opposite windows. What does this mean? A world with two suns?

The next painting, which is a "tableaux vivant," solves the enigma. An outdoor classic painting in the Greek style, a scene of Diana, the goddess of the hunt from Greek mythology. But what's this? Off to the side is a large mirror. What does it mean? Following the angle of the mirror, one sees that it is pointing directly at a basement window. The mirror is the second source of light from the first painting.

The unseen narrator and the art collector argue various interpretations. The collector seems more authoritative, and he usually has the last word. He explains the source of much of his interpretation: a novel about one of the paintings gives clues to the meaning of, not only that particular painting, but of the entire series. Yet he cautions that this is just an interpretation.

In another tableaux vivant the collector points out the poses of the human figures. Each painting has a figure whose arms are extended. Moving from one to another we can see that they trace out a curve which in imagination becomes a circle. The circles combine to form a sphere. The collector deduces that they are gestures showing the clue to divining the mystery.

From painting to painting, the collector proposes explanations and theories. One can understand his reasoning, but is it correct?—especially when he sometimes contradicts himself and rejects what he had just recently proposed.

Eventually, the collector comes to a conclusion using "The Hypothesis of the Stolen Painting" as a solution. The entire series is an occult celebration, "a revival of the cult of Mithras," and that is what caused both the scandal and the theft. The tableaux vivants were a ritual ceremony celebrating the paintings and paying homage to "Baphomet, an androgynous demon. The principle of non-definition in defiance of time. An immaculate body without soul." The collector concludes: "The enigma has been solved, certainly. And that should satisfy us. But we are not satisfied."

The weary collector ponders further possibilities, and then eventually wanders off through the maze of his museum. We expect something more to be said about the mystery of the paintings, some more definite resolution. But everything has been said, and there is only silence. The movie's conclusion is, itself, un-satisfying.

But such is life! It is a puzzle through which we attempt to piece together some vestige of meaning, some logic or interconnection that will justify all the work.

Theories and proposals abound. They can be evaluated, accepted or dismissed. We can never know for certain, for there is always that missing painting.

Director/writer Raul Ruiz and writer Pierre Klossowski have created a metaphysical labyrinth for us to visually and mentally traverse. It is the artistry of life with all its enigmas. The mystery may never be penetrated. And every conclusion remains not quite satisfying. But it is life, nevertheless, a puzzle to be continuously rearranged and solved.

As the collector (Jean Rougeul) explains at the end of his analysis:

> "I know that at this very moment . . .
> the paintings are beginning to fade
> from memory. . . ."
> ". . . So, let us forget. Let us
> allow the paintings to fade . . .
> to vanish, vanish . . . so that all
> that remains is the isolated gestures
> . . . the gestures of 'The Ceremony.'"

And, as with the paintings, so it is with life. Despite all our attempts to divine the mystery, all we have left are merely gestures, vestiges of clues that have no final resolution.

ROSENCRANTZ AND GUILDENSTERN ARE DEAD

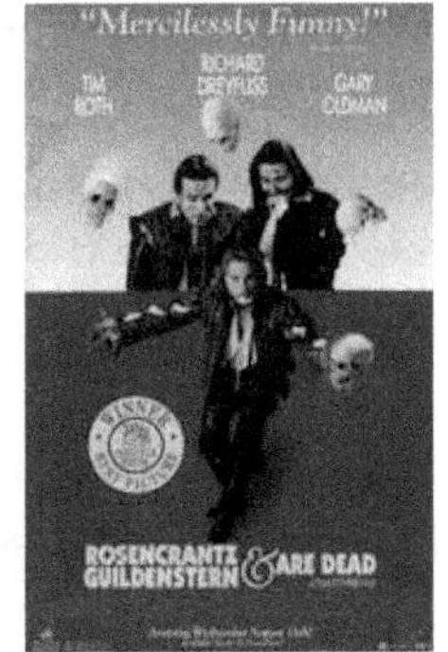

Director: Tom Stoppard
Producer: Michael Brandman &
Emanuel Azenberg
Screenplay: Tom Stoppard
From the play by Tom Stoppard
1990 Color

What is fate? What meaning does life have if it is predestined? Do our actions have any significance if we can do nothing else? Is all the world but a stage? Are we merely poor players that fret and strut our hour upon the stage, and then are heard no more?

Director/writer Tom Stoppard addresses these philosophical questions in the comic drama Rosencrantz and Guildenstern are Dead. The movie is based upon Stoppard's own play. It focuses on the two nobodies, Rosencrantz and Guildenstern, who represent the "everyman" of human life.

In Shakespeare's play, Hamlet, the two are fated to die because of an intentional misunderstanding. Stoppard follows these two along the periphery of the play. The main action in Hamlet is more or less adhered to, but the viewpoint of the two anti-heroes provides a comic play all its own.

The movie begins with Rosencrantz and Guildenstern being summoned to Elsinore Castle by the King of Denmark. However, at present, they have no idea that this has happened because both have inexplicably lost their memory. They are unconsciously being pulled by the forces of destiny via the script of Shakespeare's play.

While they are riding to court, Rosencrantz (Gary Oldman) finds a gold coin and begins flipping it heads or tails. Incredibly, each time they flip it (or any other coin), it lands heads 157 times in a row! The laws of probability seem to be in question. Fate or determinism seems to be rearing its ugly "head." It is a dark premonition of what the future holds in store.

The two ponder over the meaning and significance of such a streak. Are the laws of physics and chance being broken, or is the coin somehow being controlled? Rosencrantz assumes the role of scientific investigator. He observes nature in every detail. Like Galileo he drops a cannonball and feather from a balcony. Will they fall at the same rate? Like Newton, he is hit on the head by a falling apple: the law of gravity? He notices a pot filled with nuts hanging beside two others. As he swings one and it collides with the one beside it, he notices the others recoil from the impact: for every action there is an equal and opposite reaction. He discovers that steam-power will turn a paper pinwheel. He sits in a tub and notices that the water level rises and falls as he submerges and emerges—eureka!—Archimedes' law of volume displacement. He folds paper into an airplane and sails it through the air: the laws of aerodynamics. He observes that the natural world is determined by laws that can't be broken. Can the same be said about the world of human behavior?

Stoppard's "double-play" seems to imply that our own lives are governed by rules that cannot be broken. Rosencrantz and Guildenstern are governed by the script of a play. Periodically, throughout the movie, pages of script come fluttering out of nowhere. Everyone must follow the plot and act out the scenes.

In fact, from the very beginning their lives have been foretold. While traveling to court they meet up with the itinerant troupe of actors who will enact the play-within-a-play that enables Hamlet to "catch the conscience of the king." While out in the forest, the actors are keen on practicing their craft before an audience. They want to hone their acting skills by performing for Rosencrantz and Guildenstern.

The troupe leader (Richard Dreyfuss) gives many options for their possible performance, but Guildenstern (Tim Roth) is enticed by a play in which they themselves interact with the performers. The forest suddenly vanishes and Rosencrantz and Guildenstern find themselves in the court at Elsinore Castle. The Shakespearean play, Hamlet, begins. The movie is the interactive play that Guildenstern wished to be performed.

Stoppard is masterful in the use of witty jibes, metaphysical banter, and philosophical jousting. The central play of Hamlet is enacted in the background, protruding now and then to give form and coherence to the plot. However, the "double-play" is the real treat, for we already know the outcome of Hamlet. What we don't know is how Rosencrantz and Guildenstern, the everymen, take to their fate.

But, just like the predetermined coin-flipping at the start of the movie, there is no escaping their scripted destiny—not if the double-play is to be internally consistent with Hamlet. And so, the two anti-heroes are doomed from start to be hanged by the King of England. (Heads it is!) For Hamlet himself, who was the intended victim, had substituted the letter from the King of Denmark to the King of England to read: ". . . that on the knowing of this contents, without delay of any kind, should those bearers, Rosencrantz and Guildenstern, put to sudden death."

Rosencrantz and Guildenstern are immediately hanged. The play is over. "All the world's a stage," and Rosencrantz and Guildenstern are merely "poor players who fret and strut."

"To be, or not to be, that is the question."

"Rosencrantz and Guildenstern are dead."

GENEALOGIES OF A CRIME

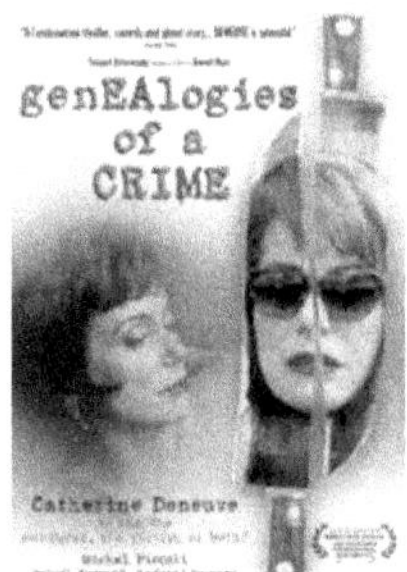

Director: Raul Ruiz
Producer: Paulo Branco
Screenplay: Raul Ruiz & Pascal Bonitzer
1998 Color
French with English subtitles

Are our lives simply variations on basic literary themes? In other words, is life just a story? Are we just characters in some novel? As situations change, do we just adapt to a different book? Are there underlying thematic structures that we follow unconsciously? If life is a fictional pattern, what book are we reading?

In Genealogies of a Crime, director/writer Raul Ruiz and writer Pascal Bonitzer attempt to delineate "the story." The movie is a profound statement about free will and destiny, as well as of the inestimable value of literature. For the number of actions and scenarios and outcomes within literature are nearly infinite. So, too, are those of humanity and human behavior. Infinite within infinite. Infinity divided by infinity. The result is a wholesome "one."

The movie begins with Solange (Catherine Deneuve), a defense attorney, who is awakened in her son's bedroom by a phone-call telling her that he has died in an accident. The same day, she takes on a case defending a young man of twenty (the same age as her son), who is accused of having murdered his aunt, Jeanne Higgins, a prominent psychoanalyst (also played by Catherine Deneuve).

Jeanne was a member of the Franco-Belgian Psychoanalytical Society whose members engaged in avant-garde forms of therapy. One bizarre exercise is the "Ceremony," involving actors and static portrayals of events in "tableaux." Another strange technique is a switching of identities: "For the next half hour, I'll be you, and you be me." It allows for each to get into the mind-set of the other. This game is played confusingly throughout the movie between Jeanne and René.

The plot of the movie is not as important as its thematic structure and philosophy. Nevertheless, it is interesting enough to relate briefly.

Solange proceeds with building a defense case. She meets René Engel (Melvil Poupaud), the young man accused of murder, and he reminds her of her dead son. He also says Solange reminds him of his aunt. Does that imply that he will kill her? She is safe if he is innocent. But if he is guilty—watch out! René claims he didn't kill his aunt, but that it was the Franco-Belgian Psychoanalytical Society that is responsible. She believes him because she wants to, and because the case is so odd. Besides, the only witness against him is "unreliable." Solange is also attracted to René, though she won't let it show.

The case continues, and René is surprisingly acquitted. This is unusual because Solange has always lost her cases. She always takes on "lost causes." The Franco-Belgian Psychoanalytical Society commits mass suicide in protest, and also because their name and credibility have been sullied. More funerals. Solange's mother has also died: another funeral. And yet another funeral as the judge dies from a third heart attack. This is truly becoming a dark comedy.

Throughout the movie the judge has been warning Solange about René. He claims René is a mastermind criminal murderer behind everything that has happened. But Solange ignores the deathbed advice.

After a respectable period, Solange takes René into her home. They become lovers. But the situation soon becomes unbearable. René always wants money. He uses Solange, and brags to his friends that he can make her do anything he wants. Solange snaps and stabs him and his two friends with a knife. She kills them all, forty stabs into René's body alone.

Now, what is fascinating about the movie is the thematic structure. From the beginning, and throughout the film, a Japanese game of "go" is shown in progress. Is life a game? Is the movie a strategy being played out? The intermittent showing of the game-board suggests such a conclusion.

The film also begins with a narrator telling the Chinese story that Solange's son had been reading when he died:

> On the 1st day of the 8th moon of Year One of the Taiyuan era of Sun Quan of Wu, a young man destined by the stars for murder killed a woman of the family of Liu Bao. A solitary woman hid him in her house.

> But she was the ghost of the woman he had killed. He fell in love with the ghost. She revealed her true identity and that her only motive was revenge.

The movie ends with the narrator repeating the same lines word for word. Sandwiched in between is Solange's meeting with the ethnopsychologist, Christian Corail, of the Société Psychanalytique de l'Ile de France, a rival group to the Franco-Belgian Psychoanalytical Society. His one peculiarity is that he relates everything in life to novels ("narrative syndrome," according to the judge investigating the Franco-Belgian group). The judge had read Christian's books on the subject and finds his theories fascinating. "Our friend believes fairy-tales are dangerous," he explains to Solange about Christian who is present with them at dinner. But Christian objects:

> . . . I said fairy-tales and stories in general act on us like illnesses or demons. You, for instance, may be one of the brothers Karamazov. And me another. Together, we can relive the novel and drag in innocent victims who will die without knowing they've been murdered by a blood-thirsty tale.
>
> I'm sorry, once I get going I can't stop, like all dreamers.

Christian realized that the murder victim, Jeanne, was re-enacting a true turn-of-the century case involving Dr. Hermine Hellmut von Hug who had also been murdered by her nephew. And Dr. Hellmut von Hug was re-enacting an 18th century Neapolitan tale, and so on . . .

Christian seems obsessed about the narrative and literary elements of life. When he next meets Solange, he remarks about the decor of her office:

> I thought the decor would be more kafkaesque. This is more Musil. No, Balzac. Part Balzac, part Akutagawa. Paul Auster without New York. Robbe-Grillet basically.

Toward the end of the movie, Christian persistently entreats Solange to visit him until she finally gives in. They meet in Christian's archives of what could be called a museum of "literary human behavior." There is an exhibit on President Kennedy as well as a Sarajevo section. According to Christian:

> There are an unlimited number of stories which have captivated Man since time began, stories which take place in various times and places. . . .
>
> According to my theory, people assume stories happen to them, actually they are possessed by stories. A few minor alterations, the story is foiled and vanishes into nothingness.

And thus, each one of us are actually characters from a novel, depending upon our situation and responses. Change one circumstance, and you're out of the novel. Some other story will suit you better.

The thematic meaning of the film is clear. Solange is acting out the oriental story framed by the beginning and ending of the movie. She is the ghost of the murdered aunt (which is why Jeanne and Solange look so much alike). She had to take revenge when René confesses he was really the murderer, and later turns her into his own plaything and puppet.

Christian Corail turns out to be the all-knowing hero of Raul Ruiz's tale. He knew what was happening on a cosmic level with Jeanne. He knew what was happening to everyone, because he was an inveterate reader of novels. He even knew what was happening to Solange, and he tried desperately to stop her before she committed the murders. When Solange sees herself in the museum as an unfinished exhibit she asks, "Am I in danger?" "Great danger," warns Christian, but to no avail.

Genealogies of a Crime is a brilliant movie by director/writer Raul Ruiz and writer Pascal Bonitzer. It is a strategic game of "go" which, though the possible responses are innumerable, they are, nevertheless, still finite. Patterns can he discerned, and though they may be complex, they are still finite and limited. In a sense, they can be considered foreordained, just like the permutations of human behavior and the possible conclusions of a novel. Though every situation and every human being is unique, there are only a set number of general patterns that our actions can follow. Life is a story that we make up as we go along. Just try not to write yourself into the character of a murderer.

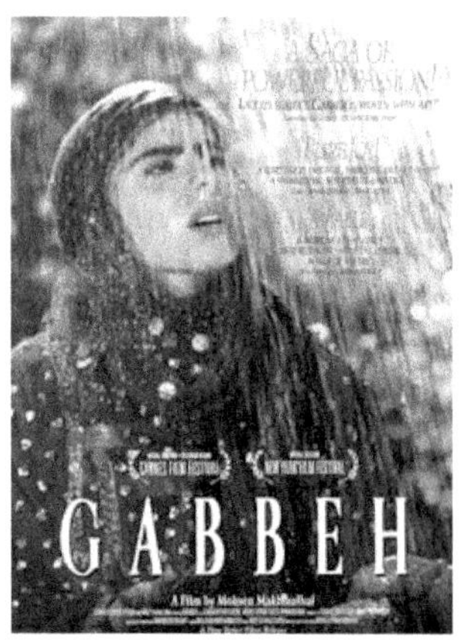

GABBEH

Director: Mohsen Makhmalbaf
Producer: Khalil Daroudchi & Khalil Mahmoudi
Screenplay: Mohsen Makhmalbaf
1996 Color
Farsi with English subtitles

Gabbeh is a colorful fable about love and the cycles of life. It is also the name of the heroine of the movie, and of the woolen carpet out of which she magically emerges. Director/writer Mohsen Makhmalbaf takes us on a magic carpet ride through time. The film is a fairy tale of self-reflective, magical realism.

The movie begins with an old couple arguing about who should wash the gabbeh in the stream. Both wish to do so, but the man wants the woman to cook while he washes. In the meantime, a pretty young girl emerges from the carpet. The old couple converse with her as they would with a neighbor, as though nothing out of the ordinary has happened. They realize who she is, for her name just happens to be Gabbeh (Shaghayegh Djodat). And her father's name is "Weave of the wool."

We see the gabbeh in the sparkling stream. Colorful figures on horseback appear through the limpid, crystal water. The girl narrates the story of her life as it emerges interwoven in the carpet.

Gabbeh is being courted by the horsemen portrayed on the gabbeh. "He had a strange voice, as if he were but an illusion." She falls in love, but her father won't allow her to marry. Delay after delay puts off the marriage he doesn't want. First, Gabbeh must wait until her uncle returns from his journey. Then, she can only marry after the uncle marries. Then, only after her mother gives birth. Her father finds endless excuses, all the while the horseman straggles behind the Ghashghai nomadic tribe, howling like a wolf on the ridgeline.

Eventually, the uncle courts a woman from another tribe, and they agree to marry. It is uncanny, for the young girl looks just like Gabbeh. And the uncle resembles a younger version of the old man.

All goes well with the married uncle. Story after story is woven into the fabric of the gabbeh: the uncle's wedding ceremony; the mother standing off to give birth; the death of Gabbeh's little sister. It is a chronicle of the family and tribe's history: a photograph album from exotic Persia.

But Gabbeh's father still won't allow her to marry. He finds excuse after excuse so that Gabbeh and her suitor consider eloping. The father has his suspicions. Gabbeh is watched day and night. Finally, the uncle offers to distract the father so that Gabbeh can escape.

The two lovers ride off over the sand dunes with the father in pursuit. He is carrying his rifle, and has always maintained that he would kill Gabbeh if she defies his will. After riding out of sight over a ridge, two shots ring out. The father rides back and dumps the gabbeh on the sand. It unrolls down the hillside. The tribe's people are stunned. Has he killed his own daughter?

The movie ends with the voice of Gabbeh saying, "My father didn't really kill us. It was only a rumor. He just said it so that my sisters wouldn't run away, and so that they never answered the wolf's call."

The viewer realizes what he knew all along. The old couple are the two young figures on horseback. Gabbeh, the young girl, is the spirit of love and romance that infuses the carpet. The gabbeh they had woven together is the tapestry of life.

Director/writer Mohsen Makhmalbaf has created a beautiful and brilliantly colorful fairy tale about life. Love is what matters. Pursue true love, and all else will follow. Gabbeh is the magic carpet ride when you follow your dreams.

CHAPTER FIVE

IMAGINATION AND ILLUSION

According to the greatest scientist of the twentieth century, "Imagination is more important than knowledge."* Einstein was referring to the materialistic emphasis on facts, figures, and quantifiable data which stifles creativity. True genius lies in the ability to dream. For a computer or encyclopedia can amass and dispense knowledge. But only man's fantasy can take the intuitive leap, linking dreams with reality in a creative mesh of thought and matter. The greatest leaps in understanding, the pivotal breakthroughs in science, were the result of imaginative insight. Perceiving reality askew, absurdly, and fancifully, is the way to understand the playful working of the universe.

---

*Albert Einstein, as quoted in "What Life Means to Einstein: An Interview by George Sylvester Viereck" in The Saturday Evening Post, 202 (26 October 1929), p. 117.

FAIL - SAFE

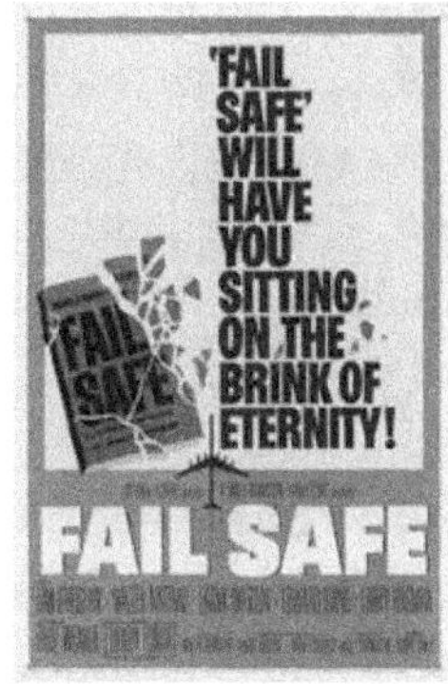

Director: Sidney Lumet
Producer: Max E. Youngstein
Screenplay: Walter Bernstein
From the novel Fail-Safe by Eugene Burdick & Harvey Wheeler
1964 B & W

Within film and literature, Fail-Safe is a classic on how illusions and counter-illusions may be necessary to safeguard reality. In this fast-paced technological society illusions hold sway and reality is held suspect. No one knows what is really true. Burdick, Wheeler, and Bernstein illustrate how confusing and distorted this network of illusions can become—just how far man has become estranged from reality. In the horrifying climax a reality must be sacrificed to placate an illusion—an illusion must be created in order to safeguard the greater reality.

The problem begins with a mechanical failure on a routine scramble bombing drill. Groups of SAC (Strategic Air Command) bombers rendezvous at points around the world. It is only a drill to test their readiness and efficiency, but because of a mechanical failure one group receives a green light to go ahead. They open their instructions, their mission: bomb Moscow. Thus an illusion, unless it is quickly rectified, is threatening all of reality—the devastation of the planet through all-out thermonuclear war.

The Strategic Air Command tries to cancel the mission, to turn the bombers around, to tell them it is an illusion. But something is wrong. They can't get through. Voice contact has been broken. The reason: the Soviets believe the attack to be real and are jamming and scrambling to disrupt communications. By proceeding as though the war-illusion is real, the Soviets themselves are consequently responsible for turning that illusion into a reality. For when the jamming of reality is ceased it is far too late: the pilots ignore the reality of peace and take it for an illusion.

On crossing the border into enemy air space SAC pilots are trained to disregard any incoming signals, especially if the message is a cancellation of the mission.

The reason is that these messages are probably illusions created by the enemy. The President himself (Henry Fonda) tries to persuade the group leader to break off the attack, but he fails. Even the wife of the group leader cannot convince him that it is a mistake. Or rather, she is convincing, he knows that it is her and not an imposter. And yet he must obey orders. He must disregard reality. Consequently SAC bomber pilots are caught up within and controlled by an illusion. Regardless of how they feel, or what they really believe, the SAC pilots are at war. They cannot turn back.

The next phase involves the technical illusions of actual warfare and the irony and insanity of mistrust and deceit. Strategic Air Command is ordered to assist Soviet Defense in shooting down the American bombers. If they fail, millions of innocent Russians will die, not to mention the probable consequences of a nuclear war.

After much reluctance and open disobedience SAC eventually cooperates. The problem now is one of sophisticated technological illusions. The bombers fly fast, can drop low to escape radar detection, and can send false images or decoys to mask their true position. The confusing illusions work only too well, for only four of the Vindicator bombers are downed. Two are left flying below radar "in the grass" with the last group of enemy fighters in pursuit. But only one of the Vindicators is armed with nuclear bombs. The unarmed "decoy" bomber re-appears on radar to distract and split the enemy forces. He is the illusion, the bait, sacrificing himself so that the armed group leader can get through. SAC urges the Soviets to ignore the decoy and go for the more obscure armed bomber, for it is the "real" threat. But the Soviet commander mistrusts the Americans and orders his fighters to engage the decoy because it is closer and an easier kill. The decoy bomber is downed and the Soviet commander collapses as he realizes his false judgment has condemned millions of his own people to death, since the real armed bomber will now almost surely get through.

The last chance for the Soviets is to create a thermonuclear barrier in front of Moscow. Using antiquated nuclear missiles they hope to create a barrage of explosions through which the bomber cannot penetrate. But the group leader is too resourceful. Once he realizes the intention, he fires his own defensive missiles straight upward in order to lure the heat-seeking missiles far away. The illusion works—the enemy missiles are led astray. The Vindicator bomber penetrates through to Moscow.

The President speaks to the Soviet Premier trying to persuade him that the attack, though now a reality, is the result of a failure, a mistake, a misunderstanding, an illusion. But simple words are not enough. In order to compensate and convince the Soviets that the attack is really an illusion, the President is forced to offer a "show" of sincerity. He must send up an American bomber which will drop two twenty-megaton bombs on New York city.

General Black is chosen to be the pilot—the executioner, the "matador" in his dream. In order to rectify the illusion of an aggressive attack on the Soviet Union, he must aggressively attack his own country, the country he has sworn his life to defend. He must destroy a concrete reality because of an illusion, a reality which just so happens to be his own reality. For his wife and children, everything he holds and loves as dear, he himself must destroy. And thus he necessarily destroys himself.

"Blackie, are Katherine and the kids in New York?" asks the President.
"Yes, sir," he answers hesitantly.
"I may be asking a great deal of you."
"I'll do whatever you say," says General Black as he leaves through swinging doors.

General Black commits suicide the moment he pushes the button and drops the bombs.

"A dream . . . a dream . . ."

And with this final act his nightmare had become real.

Thus a mechanical failure creates an illusion which results in a misunderstanding that effects reality. To rectify this misunderstanding it is necessary to create an illusion, a show of sincerity by bombing New York city. The bombing of New York is an illusion since it has no solid basis in actual reality. There is no war. U.S. planes are bombing U.S. cities. Thus it is insane and nightmarish, and yet at the same time a necessary illusion. It is an illusion enacted in order to ward off a far more dangerous real illusion—the consequences of all-out nuclear war, the probable destruction of all reality as the result of a mere illusion.

<u>Fail-Safe</u> is a prime example of how two wrongs can make a right. How a set of illusions can be a remedy to safeguard reality.

84 CHARING CROSS ROAD

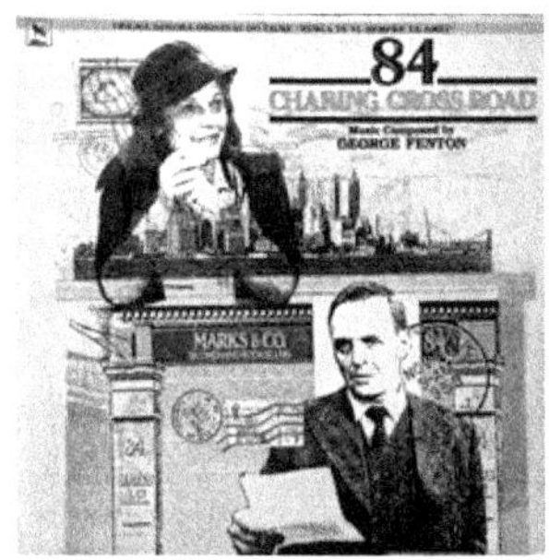

Director: David Hugh Jones
Producer: Geoffrey Helman
Screenplay: Hugh Whitemore
Based on the novel by Helene Hanff and the play by Jameo Roose-Evan
1986 Color

In 84 Charing Cross Road Helene Hanff and David Jones produce a work of fictional reality. A reality in the obvious sense that the work is based on Helene's true-life experiences. Fictional in the sense that these experiences were transposed into a book, a play, and even a movie. But more obscurely, and more importantly, it is fictional in the sense that her relationship with the people of 84 Charing Cross Road never actualized into concrete reality. Helene never made the connection to meet her friends and loves face-to-face. An incredibly meaningful and beautiful relationship has become trapped forever, crystallized in an epistolary reality.

84 Charing Cross Road is basically the true-life correspondence between Helene (Ann Bancroft) and the employees of Marks & co., Booksellers. Helene is in New York and Marks & co. is in London at 84 Charing Cross Road. Their interaction is initially a simple customer-retailer relationship. Helene wants cheap, used books on English literature which she cannot find in New York bookstores. Marks & co. provides her service, supplying her with all she needs. But over the years the relationship changes. The correspondence becomes personal. It is no longer Marks & co., but rather, Frank (Anthony Hopkins), Cecily, Megan, George, and Bill. Private messages and gossip are exchanged. They learn of each other's lives and personalities. They talk honestly and openly. But the real catalyst is Helene's generosity.

Due to postwar shortages of food and clothing, England is reduced to rationing and black-market activities. However, in America and Denmark, food and clothing are plentiful and fairly cheap. Helene begins sending little care packages and holiday presents to her favorite bookshop. The employees reciprocate by sending her a volume of love poems on her birthday and a hand-embroidered linen tablecloth for Christmas. The correspondence and book-selling continue for twenty years. It is an epistolary reality, for she never even sends her photo. Everything is left to the imagination and the written word.

Helene is well aware of the bizarre delicacy of the relationship. She fears what may happen should she meet her correspondents in the flesh. Would the magic and mystery wear off? Would they find themselves unimpressed or with nothing to say? The nature of long-distance relationships is that they are non-threatening and safe. Honesty, confession, frankness, and teasing criticism do not have to be dealt with face-to-face. One can be bolder and more blatant, and thus Helene's trepidation:

> . . . I may get to England and browse around my bookshop myself. If I have the nerve. I write them the most outrageous letters from a safe 3,000 miles away. I'll probably walk in there one day and walk right out again without telling them who i am.[1]

Helene is caught in a dilemma of contradictory desires. She wishes with all her heart to visit 84, Charing Cross Road, and yet at the same time it is something she dreads. And so she finds excuses over a twenty year time-span. First she can't go to England because she needs the money to fix her teeth. Next, she can't go because she is moving into a new apartment which needs furnishing. And finally she loses her job and just doesn't have the money.

At the same time Helene's love for her friends at Marks and Company grows, expressing itself through her openness and generosity. The employees at the antiquarian bookstore are just dying to meet her. Hopefully in some way they can return her kindness. If she would just cross the Atlantic she would find a host of eager friends. A friend of Helene's discovers this as she visits London and drops by the store.

> You might have warned us! We walked into your bookstore and said we were friends of yours and were nearly mobbed. Your Frank wanted to take us home for the weekend.
> Mr. Marks came out from the back of the store just to shake hands with friends-of-Miss-Hanff, everybody in the place wanted to wine and dine us, we barely got out alive.[2]

And so Helene's relationship with Marks and Company remains merely a correspondence, a fiction—it is never actualized into reality. The irony is that Helene cannot stomach "fiction." "I never can get interested in things that didn't happen to people who never lived."[3] And yet she herself is guilty of conspiring to keep her vicarious correspondence an English fiction. And so the inevitable happens as it does with all people over time. Cecily and Megan move away to other countries. George Martin becomes ill and dies. The old lady who made the hand-woven linen is placed in a nursing home. And one day, after twenty years, Helene is informed that Frank Doel, her main correspondent, the manager of the bookstore, her fantasy love, had a ruptured appendix and died. The owner, Mr. Marks, had died only a month before. And so, all that remains of Helene's love-relationship with 84, Charing Cross Road is a handful of letters, her memories, and her books that she has taken down and scattered lovingly all around.

> I remember years ago a guy I knew told me that people going to England find exactly what they go looking for. I said I'd go looking for the England of English literature, and he nodded and said: "It's there."
>
> Maybe it is, and maybe it isn't. Looking around the rug one thing's for sure: it's here.
>
> The blessed man who sold me all my books died a few months ago. And Mr. Marks who owned the shop is dead.[4]

The situation is irrevocable. The possibility has vanished. Through fate Helene can never meet her dear, loving friends in London—they have drifted to other realms, some have drifted into the past. The meaning has become crystallized in the form of fiction, of letters—an epistolary reality that is more real than real life. A fiction that is more real than reality itself.

Perhaps life itself is what is fleeting and unreal. The owner, the manager, the employees are gone. "But Marks & co. is still there."[5] The source of fiction and inspiration endures through time. And Helene herself begins corresponding anew with Frank Doel's children who are now adults. They want to meet her and know this person so loved by their father. The epistolary reality spans generations and becomes eternal. And the letters themselves, the medium of love, they have been transformed into a work of art—a book, a play, a movie—for all people, and for all time.

<u>84, Charing Cross Road</u> is a classic example of the art of fictional reality. Helene, a lover of English literature, turns her most meaningful reality into an English fiction—because her most meaningful fiction never became a reality.

> If you happen to pass by 84 Charing Cross Road, kiss it for me? I owe it so much.[6]

---

1 Helene Hanff, <u>84, Charing Cross Road</u> (New York: Avon Books, 1970), p. 42.
2 <u>Ibid</u>., p. 68.
3 <u>Ibid</u>., p. 44.
4 <u>Ibid</u>., p. 94.
5 <u>Ibid</u>., p. 94.
6 <u>Ibid</u>., p. 94.

HARVEY

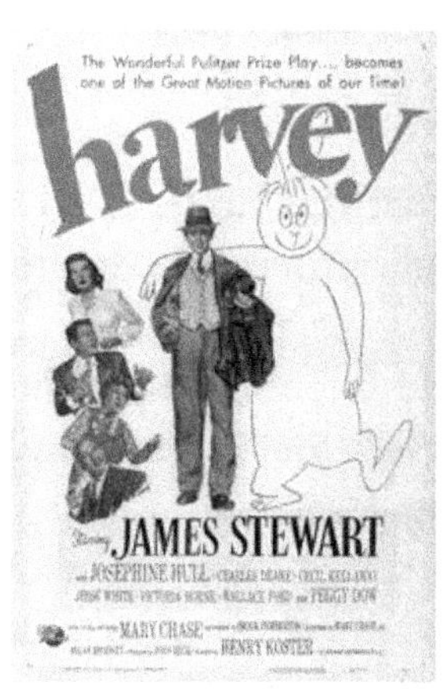

Director: Henry Koster
Producer: John Beck
Screenplay: Mary Chase & Oscar Brodney
1950 B & W
From the play by Mary Chase

Based upon the play by Mary Chase, <u>Harvey</u> is a classic, inspirational comedy. Having Jimmy Stewart as the lead character, Elwood P. Dowd, further ensures its immortality.

Elwood is a well-to-do gentleman, kind to all, with only one eccentricity: a six-foot tall rabbit who speaks to him. Now, imaginary friends are normal for children, but for an elderly respected member of the community? Elwood's sister, Veta, and niece, Myrtle Mae, won't have it. They can't even invite members of society over for lunch or tea. For Elwood insists on introducing Harvey to everyone. He even sets a place for him at the table. What would people say? Myrtle Mae's social life is in ruins. She will have no gentlemen callers. She'll become a spinster. The family will be the laughing-stock of the community. And so . . . Veta and her daughter decide to have Elwood committed.

The theme is typical: those who don't conform must be extracted and contained. But Elwood's only crime is talking to a six-foot tall rabbit. It is a harmless aberration. And yet, he is to be injection-shocked into docility so that his sister and niece won't be embarrassed, so that they can have members of social standing over for tea.

A madcap chase ensues. Veta, instead of Elwood, is mistakenly committed to the asylum. Elwood is finally tracked down and persuaded to return and take her place. He also reluctantly agrees to the injection shock therapy, if only to please Veta.

"You know, we all must face reality, Dowd, sooner or later,"
says Doctor Sanderson.
"Well, I wrestled with reality for thirty-five years, Doctor. And
I'm happy to state, I finally won out over it."

Now that Veta has regained control, she begins to have second thoughts. Doubts and guilt prompt her to stop the treatments before they begin. A taxi driver demands payment before the treatments are started, because "they change them in there." The patients are nice and generous before the treatment, but afterwards they're mean and stingy. He'd be lucky to get a tip. Beforehand the patients talked and watched the birds and the sunsets. "Sometimes they even watched birds that weren't there and sunsets when it was raining." Afterwards the taxi driver is treated as a mere servant, lucky to even be employed. No sir, he wants his money now!

Veta is now convinced. She wants Elwood to remain his "normal" self—his kind, gentle, generous self. Why, dealing with Harvey wasn't so bad. She admits, accidentally, to even liking Harvey (for at times, she too has seen and talked to him).

Elwood P. Dowd has been saved. Man's imaginative and creative capacity (for such is what Harvey represents) will be given safe harbor. Harvey is actually the saving grace of mankind, for without him we become the dull and lifeless automatons of the social order. Harvey embodies the playful, creative, childhood possibilities. He is the trickster, the pooka, the mischievous prankster of Celtic mythology. He is what set man dreaming about walking upon the moon. He is the wellspring of art, music, and literature. He embraces the eccentricity that makes us unique.

On some subtle level, even Veta herself knows what Harvey represents. For while lecturing Doctor Chumly, she is standing unknowingly in front of Elwood's seated portrait which has Harvey standing behind him.

"The photograph shows only the reality.

The painting shows not only the reality, but the dream behind it. It's our dreams, doctor, that carry us on."

Mary Chase fully deserves the accolades for her Pulitzer prize-winning play. For Harvey embodies the American ideal of individuality and imagination—the necessary requisites for creating a dream.

Behind every great man stands an ideal. And, there, behind Elwood, stands a six-foot tall rabbit named Harvey.

BIG FISH

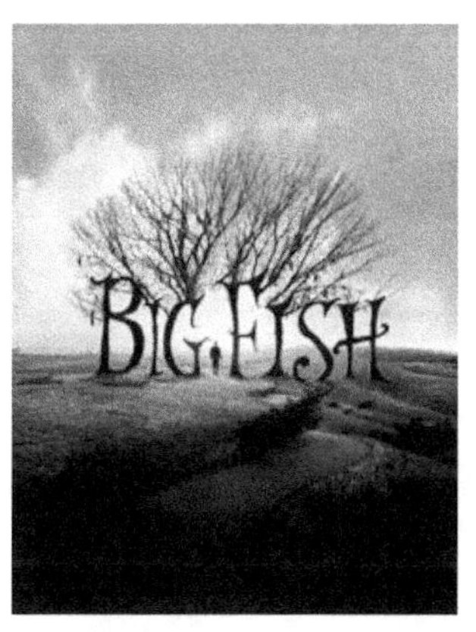

Director: Tim Burton
Producer: Richard D. Zanuck, Bruce Cohen & Dan Jinks
Screenplay: John August
From the novel by Daniel Wallace,
Big Fish, A Story of Mythic Proportions
2003 Color

The storyteller is revered in most cultures, especially those with no written language. For it was the only way to pass cultural history from generation to generation. Even cultures possessing written language hold the storyteller in high esteem. For he is an entertainer who mesmerizes the family and tribe. Without television, how else to distract children and adults through the dark night? And what better way to bond than through imagination?

In Big Fish, director Tim Burton and writers John August and Daniel Wallace portray the life of a modern-day storyteller—one of the last of a dying breed. Ed Bloom (Albert Finney) is shown to be a lovable, life-of-the-party teller of tall tales. He is the epitome of the "big fish" exaggerators who is so convincing that he even believes his own lies. For the best liar is the one who believes he speaks the truth.

The movie begins, more or less, at his son's wedding banquet. Ed Bloom is once again telling tall tales to entertain the guests. Will (Billy Crudup) is incensed that his father is stealing the show. The crowd loves him, but this is Will's night. He confronts his dad later about all his showboating lies. They argue, and Will and Ed don't speak to each other for three years.

Will receives a phone call from his mother. His father is dying. The doctors have given up hope. Will and his wife fly out to spend the last remaining days with his parents. The dying is a slow process, drawn out long enough so that Will can question his dad and resolve their differences.

Will claims he just wants to know the truth. His wife is pregnant, and he wants his son to know him just as he should know his own father—something other than exaggerations or outright lies. Will is upset that he, himself, doesn't really know his own father. He knows all the stories, certainly (he's heard them a thousand times), but he doesn't know how to separate fact from fiction.

"You're like Santa Claus and the Easter Bunny combined—just as charming, and just as fake."

"You think I'm fake?"

"Only on the surface, Dad. But it's all I've ever seen. . . ."

"Who do you want me to be?" asks Ed.

"Just yourself," implores Will. . . . Ed is taken aback.

"I've been nothing but myself since the day I was born. And if you can't see that, it's your failing, not mine."

Will is demoralized and dismayed. Even as he lies dying, his father refuses to be honest. He's still hiding behind his facade.

The story-telling of the movie is told in larger-than-life flashbacks. With the aura of myth and legend, Ed (the younger: Ewan McGregor) relates his astonishing adventure through life: tales of witches, giants, and werewolves; of finding a magical town called Spectre; and of joining up with the circus. He tells the fairy-tale romance of courting his wife (the love of his life to whom he had always remained faithful); the unbelievable war story of escaping from North Korea with the help of beautiful Siamese-twin singers; the drama of a daring bank robbery that results in a Wall Street tycoon becoming his benefactor. Ed's life certainly has more zest and flavor than that of most ordinary mortals.

Time takes its toll. Ed Bloom has a stroke and lies dying in a hospital bed. But he must pass on the story-telling tradition to a matter-of-fact non-believer. His dying wish is to hear about his vision of death seen within the Witch's glass eye. "I don't know that story, Dad. You never told me that one," objects Will, always matter-of-fact. But Ed's pleading eyes convince Will to tell it anyway—the way he sees it.

Will knows how important this moment is to his father. Falteringly, but with growing excitement, Will throws himself into full storyteller mode. After all, he has learned from the Master. He's had a lifetime apprenticeship.

Will tells how his father's strength has suddenly returned. He demands to leave the hospital, and so Will sets him in a wheelchair. They bust out and are pursued through the halls by orderlies, doctors, and guards. Will drives him down to the river where it is like a festive baptism. All Ed's friends are there, even those who have died. Everybody is cheerful and ecstatic. It is like a birthday party for the beginning of a new life.

Will carries his father out into the river and releases him. When he submerges there is magic. Ed turns into the "Big Fish" of his own story, and swims delightfully away.

Ed Bloom dies peacefully with a smile on his face. His son has given him all he ever wanted—a beautiful story that he had invented on his own. The prodigal son returns to carry on the faith of his father—the ancient religion of the myth-maker.

The funeral is held, and lo and behold, who should appear? A giant, a midget, a bank-robber, circus men, and oriental twins. It is a joyous gathering, as they all congregate to exchange stories about Ed. The stories may have been exaggerated, but they all had a basis in fact. The so-called "lies" were actually somewhat true.

Big Fish is a modern-day parable about the importance of imagination. In a hard-fact society, the ability to imagine is sadly lacking. Director Tim Burton and writers John August and Daniel Wallace have imagined a fairy tale of mythical proportions. Ed Bloom's life was truly a marvelous adventure. What difference does it make what percentage of his story was real? For he entertained everyone he met; he made them silly and happy; he distracted them from everyday factual concerns. He imbued life with magic and mystery, and endowed it with a mythical reverence. And that is why he was so well-loved.

"The man tells his stories so many times that he becomes the stories.

They live on after him—and in that way he becomes immortal."

DREAMKEEPER

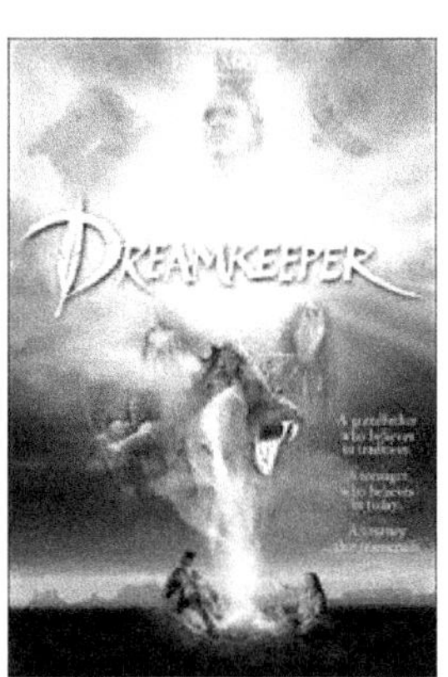

Director: Steve Barron
Producer: Matthew O'Connor & Ron McLeod
Screenplay: John Fusco
2003 Color

"Does it matter if the stories are no longer told?—if there's no one to keep the dream?"

Folktales, myths, and legends embody the soul of a people. One's culture and heritage are distilled in an exciting, entertaining, and educational form. The storyteller passes on the beliefs and values through the art of imaginative oratory and pantomime. Each generation thus absorbs and refines the ancestral dream. But what if there are no more storytellers? What if storytelling becomes a dying art?

Dreamkeeper explores these matters in a beautiful epic movie three hours long. Director Steve Barron and writer John Fusco show the culture of Native Americans through a series of their own myths. The meaning of each tribe's history is distilled in legends and fables. The movie displays each story as featurette films within a film—flashbacks into the ancestral past.

The plot of the movie begins with Shane (Eddie Spears), an angry, troubled, seventeen-year-old boy on the Pine Ridge Indian Reservation in South Dakota. His father abandoned the family for alcohol long ago. Shane's mother raised him with the help of "Old Pete Chasing Horse" (August Schellenberg), the eighty-six-year-old grandfather who wants to pass on his storytelling craft before he dies.

Shane is in trouble with the local gang, as well as with his girlfriend. His Mom wants him to drive Old Pete cross-country to the All Nations Powwow. His grandfather is getting old. He wants to tell his tales one more time, and offer up his old horse in the ceremonial "give away."

The Indian gang is after Shane, and the relationship with his girlfriend is on ice. Shane figures the trip would be a temporary escape, although he really has no interest in his grandfather or the powwow. He is a modern Lakota bored with his heritage. His only interest is in getting into trouble.

To pass the time on the long drive, Old Pete tells stories from various Native American tribes: Lakota, Blackfoot, Kiowa, Sioux, Mohawk, and Pawnee. For the stories belong to all Native Americans. They are the heart and soul of the Indian people.

One Lakota story is that of High Horse who strives to win the hand of the chief's daughter, Bluebird Woman. High Horse is rejected again and again by the chief. In suicidal despair he throws himself at the enemy Crow encampment. Surprisingly, he scares them all away and returns with a herd of their horses. The chief now accepts the marriage of High Horse and Bluebird Woman. He explains that what he wanted was not ponies, but rather a man who was "a doer of great deeds."

Other myths and legends are interspersed throughout the three-hour movie. Grandfather relates these tales to break the monotony—and also to seduce Shane into the art of storytelling.

One Mohawk myth is that of "Thunderboy and Skywoman." An Indian maiden marries the Thunderspirit who truly loves her, because he will love her more than any mortal on earth. A Kiowa legend of "The Red-Headed Indian" is supposedly based on fact. Although kidnapped from the white man and raised as an Indian warrior, Tayhan proves himself a true Kiowa and dies defending his people. A Pawnee folktale is of "Dirty Belly and the Dun Pony." It exemplifies the notion that appearances are not always what they seem. A Northern Cheyenne myth of

"Quillwork Girl" is about the creation of the Big Dipper. A Northwest Pacific story is of the willing sacrifice of a chief's daughter to make the tribe's illness go away. And everyone's favorite: the trickster tales of Coyote and Iktomi the Spider.

Each of these vignettes has a moral: courage, honesty, tolerance, and loyalty. Each embodies the wisdom accrued over centuries. The storytellers are the means through which this knowledge is passed from one generation to the next.

The Lakota legend of "Eagle Boy and his Vision Quest" parallels Shane's own journey of self-discovery. It takes place one-thousand years in the past and is told in sequels throughout the movie. Eagle Boy embarks on his quest, praying for four days and nights without food or water. He must conquer his fears, learn patience and discipline.

Eagle Boy's bravery and skills are tested when he meets and defeats a water dragon. A medicine woman advises him to cut out the dragon's heart in order to gain wisdom and power. Eagle Boy does so, and from then on his arrows never miss. He can have any woman he wants. He achieves wealth and status among his tribe. In short, he embodies the North American Indian version of Faust.

But things are too easy. Eagle Boy grows weary of his power and prestige. Finally, out of despair, he admits: "I just want to be like other men." He exposes the magic Serpent heart to the eyes of the tribe. Its power vanishes, and all that he is left with is an ordinary rock. Eagle Boy flings away the rock in disgust. In a magical transposition he is once again back on the mountain in search of his vision. He is still in his sacred prayer circle, still on his four-day-long quest. Was all that had happened only delirium and dream?

And yet, perhaps the vision has been given, although Eagle Boy does not yet understand. He has glimpsed the emptiness and vanity for which most people strive. And yet, he is only an adolescent boy. He must nurture this wisdom to truly become a man.

The moral: power, greed, and pride are devoid of meaning. Eagle Boy realizes that the meaning of life is just in living.

And now, back to the larger "picture." The cross-country trip eventually ends at the trailer-home of Shane's father. It was a Trickster trick! Old Pete just wanted Shane reconciled with his father (Pete's own son).

Anger and resentment are all that Shane now feels. But the unexpected (or expected) happens and Old Pete takes the great journey overnight. Sadness and mourning replace Shane's hostility. In a strange way, the grandfather's death has brought the father and son together. The old storyteller trickster knew it all along. The death of this old man has forged a bond between generations—just as had his storytelling life.

The father decides to drive Old Pete's body back to the reservation for burial. Shane chooses to take the old horse to the All Nation's Powwow. It is the least he can do. It is what Grandfather would have wanted.

The structure of the movie is completed as Shane arrives at the festive powwow. All the mythological characters appear in their modern guise. There is Dirty Belly and the Red-Headed Indian. Over there is Quillwork Girl, Thunderboy, and Bluebird Woman. The legend is an undercurrent through each generation of the people.

Shane presents Grandfather's horse to a woman who knew Old Pete. But the circle isn't completed until the final scene: children gather around Shane who sits drumming the tom-tom underneath a tree. He begins telling the stories that he learned from his grandfather—the stories handed down from ancient times. Now Shane has become the new storyteller, passing on the tribe's history to an even younger generation. His father and grandfather would have been proud.

Dreamkeeper is indeed what its name implies. The storyteller protects the dreams of his people. He disseminates them, like seeds, at each story-gathering for all to absorb, cherish, and enjoy.

Director Steve Barron and writer John Fusco have created an inspirational epic about Native American mythology. But it is not just about legends. It is about the cultural pride in embracing one's heritage. It is about the meaning passed on through the storytelling tradition. And it is about the bonds between grandfather, father, and son.

In a symbolic finale, the movie closes with an overhead view of the All Nations Powwow. Pulling back farther and farther, the dancers in a circle form a design that merges into the pattern on the shell of a turtle. In Indian mythology the entire earth is supported on the back of the Great Turtle. The turtle's shadowy form swims off slowly into the depths of the sea.

CHAPTER SIX

VIRTUAL REALITY

With the advent of computer-generated, virtual reality a new avenue of experience opens before man. No longer do pilots, soldiers, and astronauts have to pay for their mistakes. For they can be trained in simulators with programs that will hone their skills. The school of hard knocks can be "virtually" softened. But the problem arises when technology creates programs difficult to distinguish from reality. At what point does the game become too real?

The question has both philosophical and metaphysical ramifications. For in the future we may not be able to differentiate. What meaning can be attributed to human experience when it is virtual? Does the soul learn and progress, or is it hampered and regressed? The final question may be, "does it make any difference?" For perhaps reality, itself, is only "virtually" real.

TOTAL RECALL

Director: Paul Verhoeven
Producer: Buzz Feitshans & Ronald Shusett
Screenplay: Ronald Shusett, Dan O'bannon & Gary Goldman
From the short story "We can Remember It for You Wholesale" by Phillip K. Dick
1990 Color

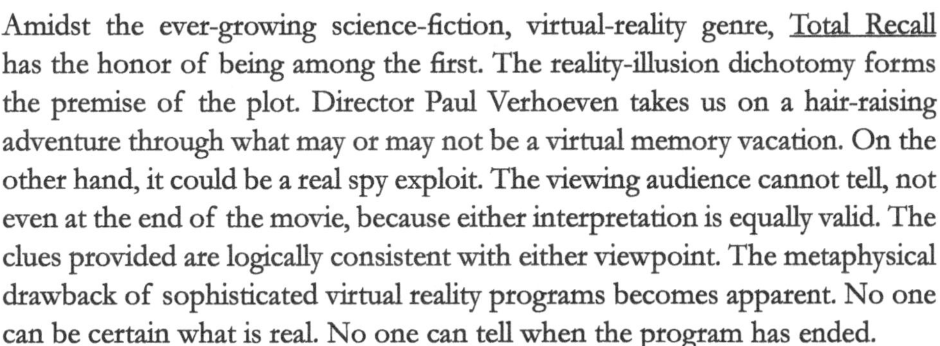

Amidst the ever-growing science-fiction, virtual-reality genre, Total Recall has the honor of being among the first. The reality-illusion dichotomy forms the premise of the plot. Director Paul Verhoeven takes us on a hair-raising adventure through what may or may not be a virtual memory vacation. On the other hand, it could be a real spy exploit. The viewing audience cannot tell, not even at the end of the movie, because either interpretation is equally valid. The clues provided are logically consistent with either viewpoint. The metaphysical drawback of sophisticated virtual reality programs becomes apparent. No one can be certain what is real. No one can tell when the program has ended.

The movie begins with construction worker, Doug Quaid (Arnold Schwarzenegger), waking up from a nightmare about Mars. Although he has never been there, he dreams of it every night. Doug decides to take a two-week virtual reality vacation from a company called "Total Recall." For a price they will implant a manufactured memory of Mars. For only a little more, they will give Quaid a new identity to go with the memory. As the salesman persuades in his pitch:

> "No matter where you go, there you are. It's always the same old you.
> Let me suggest that you take a vacation from yourself."

Quaid is sold on the "Ego Trip." He chooses the option "Secret Agent":

> "You are a top operative back under deep cover on your most important mission. People are trying to kill you left and right.

> You meet this beautiful, exotic woman . . . but you rest assured, by the time the trip is over you get the girl, kill the bad guys, and save the entire planet."

Quaid is intrigued and eagerly accepts. In no time he is in the laboratory having his memory-implant installed. But something goes wrong. The doctor says he's having a "schizoid embolism." Quaid goes berserk trying to get free. He is a different person. He accuses the doctors of ruining everything. They popped his memory-cap, and now all hell will break loose.

In panic, the doctors at Total Recall sedate him and wipe his memory of the event. When he awakens in a cab, he has no idea what's been happening. A co-worker has to tell him that he went on a vacation at Total Recall.

The co-worker and his cohorts then try to capture or kill Quaid, but Quaid kills them all. When he returns to his apartment his wife Lori (Sharon Stone) also tries to kill him. After a knock-down-drag-out she finally admits the truth. Quaid himself is a phony construct of false memories. That's all she knows. But he finds out later that, after working for the mining agency that governs Mars, Quaid double-crossed Cohaagen (the head of the corporation). In an attempt to silence him, the agency had his memory erased and sent him back to earth with a false life and wife. She, herself, also works for Cohaagen, and was hired to keep a close watch on Quaid. "I'm sorry Quaid, your whole life is just a dream."

More twists and turns of the plot. Quaid goes to Mars for the first time, or had he been there before? He joins the underground resistance to the mining agency. Many of its members have been deformed and mutated because of lack of environmental regulations.

Quaid discovers Melina (Rachel Ticotin), the brunette he's been dreaming about every night. She knows him as Hauser, Quaid's alter-ego from the past. It is hard to believe that Hauser is now Quaid, but eventually she is convinced.

Meanwhile, Quaid is greeted by a knock on his door. It is a doctor from Total Recall who claims that Quaid has had a psychotic break. This is all an illusion. They are really back on earth at Total Recall. His wife, all nice and concerned, joins the two in the "apparent" apartment. She tries to convince Quaid to take the doctor's antidote and come back down to earth. They are both convincing. For, after all, this is the exact theme of the Secret Agent vacation.

Quaid almost complies when he notices perspiration rolling down the doctor's cheek. Why is he nervous, if none of it's real? If the gun Quaid is pointing at him is an illusion, then it doesn't matter if he pulls the trigger. He does so. The doctor dies. Lori's evil nature erupts as she, along with the agency, captures and beats Quaid.

Melina comes to the rescue and takes Quaid to meet Kuato, the leader of the resistance. He is a mutant baby-like being attached to the belly and chest of another man. Perhaps the most insightful and meaningful advice comes from this sage-baby:

"What do you want, Mr. Quaid?" asks Kuato.

"The same as you, to remember."

"But why?"

"To be myself again."

"You are what you do. A man is defined by his action—not his memory."

And so, it doesn't really matter if Quaid was really Hauser who had a different agenda. He is now Quaid, and can interact as such. He is his own man. What may have happened in the past is meaningless. It's what happens right now that counts. Or, as the saying goes: "Today is the first day of the rest of your life."

But what happens now? The underground has been penetrated and overthrown by soldiers of the mining conglomerate. Kuato is shot dead. Quaid has unknowingly lead them to Kuato and broken the resistance.

Now Quaid is taken back to Cohaagen's office. A tape is shown of Hauser gloating about what he has accomplished. The suppression of Hauser, the creation of Quaid—it was all, from day one, merely an attempt to penetrate the rebel underground. And now Hauser wants to come back.

Both Quaid and Melina are taken to the laboratory to have their memories erased and new ones implanted. Quaid will become Hauser if the experiment is not stopped. He breaks free, kills the scientists, and saves Melina. They then attempt to restart an alien atmospheric machine that will provide oxygen for the whole planet. The inhabitants will thus be freed from the stranglehold on oxygen by the mining syndicate.

Cohaagen tries to stop them at the last minute. He has the drop on Quaid, and can't resist casting aspersions which impugn Quaid's character and his very being:

"You had to be Quaid."

"I am Quaid," says Quaid defiantly.

"You're nothing. You're nobody.
You're a stupid dream. Well, all dreams come to an end."

He is about to fire his gun when, at the last moment, Melina shoots Cohaagen.

The generators work. Mars' atmosphere is filled with oxygen. It's like paradise. Everyone can breathe freely, unrestrained by the artificial dome.

"I can't believe it. It's like a dream," says Melina in awe.
"What's wrong?" she asks Quaid, who has a dour expression.

"I just had a terrible thought.
What if this is a dream?"

For a simple, action-packed, science-fiction thriller, Total Recall has some surprisingly profound insights. As Kuato counseled Quaid: "You are what you do. A man is defined by his action—not his memory."

And Quaid, "a stupid dream," according to Cohaagen, was nevertheless successful in overthrowing the oppressive mining corporation. He saved the planet and won the beautiful girl. But wasn't that precisely the "Secret Agent" program of Total Recall? I'm not exactly certain. I can't really recall. Oh well, remembering the past doesn't matter. It's how we respond now that counts.

End program?

eXistenZ

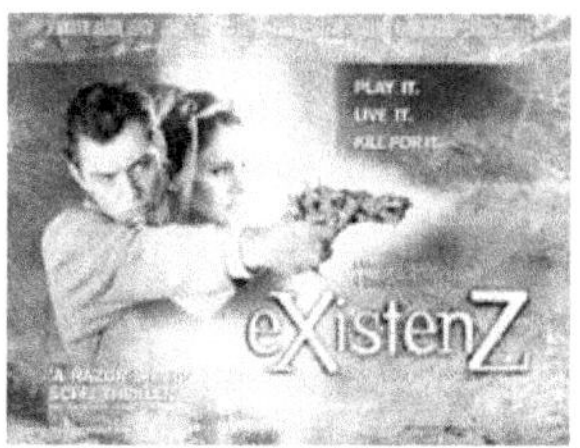

Director: David Cronenberg
Producer: David Cronenberg, Robert Lantos, & Andras Hamori
Screenplay: David Cronenberg
1999 Color

The greatest game is the one that appears to be real. The more realistic, the more intense, the more the adrenaline rush. If a scenario appears phony, it soon becomes boring. It lacks excitement. Therefore, realism in every detail is the ideal form of entertainment. By fooling both the body and the mind, the best game is indistinguishable from reality. And therein lies the greatest achievement and the greatest pitfall of "eXistenZ."

Director/writer David Cronenberg creates the ultimate world of games—a world where playing and pretense may bleed over into real life. A point must be reached when the player finally wakes up. But which reality is real? Or is it just another game?

The movie begins at a virtual-reality game seminar. The greatest game designer in the world, Allegra Geller (Jennifer Jason Leigh), a goddess in the industry, is premiering her newest game: "eXistenZ."

The game software is downloaded from Allegra's master-pod into slave-pods of the twelve other volunteers. From those pods, umbilical cords plug into "bio-ports" previously installed into the spinal cords of each person. It is a futuristic world where game-playing is taken to the extreme. Tapping directly into the human nervous system, these games manipulate the brain into sensing a world of virtual reality.

As the seminar game is just beginning, a man from the audience steps forward with an alien-looking weapon and fires at Allegra, striking her in the shoulder. "Death to the demoness, Allegra Geller!" Pandemonium breaks out. People scream and run from the room. The head of the seminar is also shot. "Death to Antenna Research!" While lying injured he urges his trainee, security guard, Ted Pikul (Jude Law), to flee with Allegra. There may be more terrorists. Meanwhile, two other guards pull guns and shoot to death the attempted assassin.

Ted evacuates Allegra from the building and drives her away. They are on the run throughout the movie. No one can be trusted. There are probably hostile elements even inside Antenna Research, itself.

Ted fixes Allegra's wound, but she is more concerned about her master-pod. It contains the only existing software for "eXistenZ." And it may have been injured during the foray. The only way to assess the damage is to play it with a friendly partner. However, Ted has no "bio-port." He gets one installed by a double-crossing gas station attendant (Willem Dafoe). The gas man tries to kill Allegra because there is a five million dollar bounty on her head. But Ted saves the day by playing his role as security guard and killing the gas man.

They then find refuge with an old, Antenna Research friend of Allegra's. He provides Ted with a good bio-port and now they can play the game. The two enter an alternate universe of secret agents and nefarious organizations. Paranoia runs rife. The game grows too complex. It begins mimicking reality. For in the game there are also people out to kill Allegra. They are the "realists" who believe Allegra and Antenna Research are subverting reality.

> "I don't like it here," says Ted with trepidation while inside the game. "I don't know what's going on. We're both stumbling around together in this unformed world whose rules and objectives are largely unknown, seemingly indecipherable, or even possibly non-existent—always on the verge of being killed by forces that we don't understand."
>
> "That sounds like my game, all right," says Allegra with delight.
>
> "That sounds like a game that's not going to be easy to market."
>
> "But it's a game everybody's already playing."

For it's the game of life. And eXistenZ is mimicking life to perfection. The game continues with many twists of plot, till no one is certain what is real. Even after pausing eXistenZ and temporarily exiting the game, Ted is still troubled. "I'm not sure here, where we are, is real at all. This feels like a game to me. And you, you're beginning to feel a bit like a game character."

The game is paralleling reality to an uncanny degree. In an apparent climax to the game, Allegra shoots her old friend from Antenna Research. For he betrayed her, and she believes it is all just part of the script. But Ted is shocked: "Allegra, what if we're not in the game anymore? . . . If we're not, then you just killed someone real."

However, to everyone's delight the game does end—or does it? They revive and awaken in the seminar, but with a different seminar leader and game designer. It turns out that Ted is just a volunteer-player who was playing a security guard. And Allegra? Allegra is also just a volunteer-player who was playing the designer of "eXistenZ"—which, it turns out, was only a scripted fabrication. The real game they were playing was "transCendenZ," and the corporation wasn't Antenna Research, it was PilgrImage.

It was an intense and incredible experience. But the game designer and seminar leader are worried. The game was interactive between the software and each of the twelve volunteers. And there was definitely a powerful "anti-game" theme to the script—a "realist" paranoid streak. Are some of the players members of the "realist" underground? Their suspicion is confirmed when they are confronted by Ted and Allegra:

> "Yevgeny, don't you think you should have to suffer for all the harm you've done and intend to do to the human race?" demands Allegra.
>
> "What?" asks Yevgeny in bewilderment.
>
> "Yes," declares Ted. "Don't you think the world's greatest game artist ought to be punished for the most effective deforming of reality?"
>
> Both Ted and Allegra then pull out their guns, shooting Yevgeny and the seminar leader till they're dead.
>
> "Death to the demon, Yevgeny Neurish!"
>
> "Death to PilgrImage! Death to transCendenZ!"

They then turn and point their weapons at another of the volunteer-players. He is frightened and confused. "No, no, no, no . . . You don't have to shoot me," he pleads. And then, almost as an afterthought: "Hey, tell me the truth. Are we still in the game?"

The movie screen goes blank, and after an interminable pause, the credits roll. Metaphysical chills are sent up and down one's "bio-ported" spine. "Are we still in the game?" The inability to distinguish a complex game from a complex reality is a philosophically profound dilemma.

David Cronenberg has created a masterpiece in the virtual reality genre. If a game mimics reality too successfully, as all games strive to do, then reality and pretense begin to blur. The "realist" underground who seemed such ruthless terrorists, may actually be justified in their radical extremism. For the undermining of reality is the greatest of all threats to mankind.

The subtle, uncomfortable, and yet poignant question necessarily arises: "Are we still in the game?" Perhaps we have always been playing the game. Perhaps life itself is the ultimate game that we take so seriously to be real. Perhaps one day, perhaps at death, we will awaken to reality and the truth. Perhaps what we are engaged in now is mere "eXistenZ."

THE THIRTEENTH FLOOR

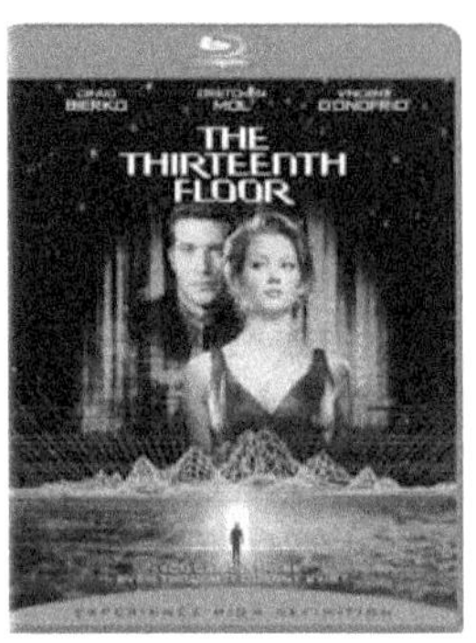

Director: Joseph Rusnak
Producer: Roland Emmerich, Ute Emmerich & Marco Weber
Screenplay: Joseph Rusnak & Ravel Centeno-Rodriguez
From the novel Simulacron-3 by Daniel F. Galouye
1999 Color

"I think, therefore I am."

Descartes

What happens when computer programs become so sophisticated that they achieve self-awareness? It is the holy grail of Artificial Intelligence researchers. It is the nemesis of philosophers trying to define consciousness and the parameters of free will. In The Thirteenth Floor, director Joseph Rusnak and writer Daniel Galouye explore an infinite regress of virtual-reality cyber-beings that become aware of their role as programs. What meaning and purpose can be attributed to illusions that can think?

The movie begins with Hannon Fuller, the genius head of a virtual reality corporation, moving through his 1937 L.A. virtual program. He leaves a letter with a bartender addressed to Douglas Hall, his executive officer next in line for inheriting the corporation. Fuller comes back to modern real life and tries to reach Hall. Instead, he is viciously murdered—stabbed to death over and over.

Douglas Hall (Craig Bierko) is awakened in the morning by a detective's message asking him to call back. He notices his bloody clothes, and yet he can't remember a thing. The detective has his suspicions, but also has no proof.

At the laboratory the head computer whiz, Whitney (Vincent D'Onofrio), sends Hall into Fuller's virtual reality program. The mystery of his murder must lie somewhere inside this 1937 L.A. scenario. For Fuller was just there. His phone message to Hall had been urgent. "Something incredible" must be explained.

Douglas Hall is impressed. It is his first time inside the program, and it is unbelievably convincing. It's another city, another universe within a computer!

Hall goes on a private investigation of all the characters that Fuller had contacted. Eventually, after his second trip into 1937 L.A., he discovers that the letter (addressed to him) had been left with the bartender; and that the bartender had read it; and that he had followed its instructions to the letter: he had driven to the outskirts of town and just kept going. He ignored signs and warnings, and even broke through barriers. And now he knows that he's not real. He realizes that he's just a character in someone else's fiction.

The discovery makes him belligerent and hostile. "I want to know why. Why would you put us through this? Why you fucking with our minds?" He fights with Hall, and even shoots him twice with a gun. "Is this real?" he laughs as Hall writhes in agony. He doesn't mind causing pain, because he doesn't like others toying with his life. "How do you like having your life fucked with?"

Previously, in the real world, Hall had met Jane Fuller, the daughter of the murdered corporate head. She tells him her father wanted to shut down the company. He was worried. Things weren't right. Later, Jane disappears. The detective says, Fuller never had a daughter. Hall tracks Jane to a small grocery store. But she doesn't even recognize him. Something is not right. Hall begins to realize the truth.

Hall jumps in his car and begins driving relentlessly to the outskirts of town. He keeps on driving, ignoring signs and barricades. Eventually he sees exactly what the bartender had seen. He sees what Fuller had instructed him to see by following the letter. He is standing by his car overlooking a valley filled with grid patterns like a giant game-board. He himself is inside a virtual program even though he is supposedly in modern time, modern L.A. He is outside the 1937 L.A. of the bartender. And yet he is still inside a game.

Fuller wanted him to realize that he and Hall were themselves merely virtual programs, and that modern L.A. was also a program. But who were the real programmers? What was the real reality? What was the real time?

Jane Fuller contacts Hall. She is no longer Jane Fuller or the check-out girl, but someone from the future 2024 L.A. She explains that the virtual beings were never supposed to become conscious of the game. There are thousands of simulations. "But yours is the only one that ever created a simulation within the simulation."

Fuller's experiments in virtual reality had caused a paradoxical effect, and he had become conscious. He contaminated the program by telling Hall and, inadvertently, the snoopy bartender. Now, even the police detective has become aware of the illusion.

The plot approaches a climax when Hall takes the place of Jane's husband in 2024 L.A. It is beautiful and other-worldly. It is an alien paradise with futuristic architecture. Jane and Hall can live out their fantasy love and shut down the game program forever. But as they are basking in the glowing sunset and their future potential love, the image on the screen suddenly compresses to a horizontal line. The audience sees the bright line contract to a bright point in the center, and then flick off. The screen goes dark. Even 2024 L.A. was merely a program. Hence, the title of Galouye's novel: Simulacron-3.

The Thirteenth Floor creates a "Chinese box" of virtual programs and virtual beings who have attained self-awareness. The unsettling question posed is the validity of our own existence. Are we merely virtual beings in a virtual program whose ultimate designer may just happen to be God?

"These people are real.

They are as real as you and me."

VANILLA SKY

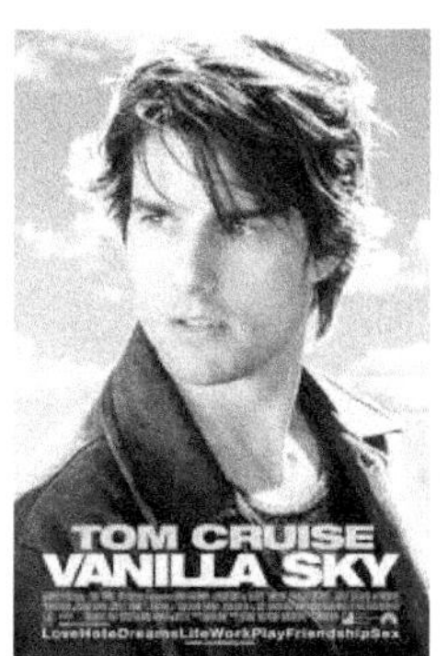

Director: Cameron Crowe
Producer: Tom Cruise, Paula Wagner & Cameron Crowe
Screenplay: Cameron Crowe
Based on the 1997 Spanish film Open Your Eyes directed by Alejandro Amenabar & Mateo Gil
2001 Color

What is better: a happy dream or a harsh reality? Given the choice between a pleasant world of illusions or ugly disfigurement and lost love—which is more appealing? Are we ever really in love with another person, or merely in love with our ideal image of them? At any moment can we change the whole direction of our lives? These philosophical questions are addressed in the science-fiction thriller Vanilla Sky.

Vanilla Sky is a remake of the Spanish movie Open Your Eyes. Normally, credit and commentary would be reserved for the original. However, Vanilla Sky is more meaningful in a philosophical and ethical sense. The last scene on the rooftop is also more emotionally poignant. And yet, Vanilla Sky would not exist if not for Open Your Eyes. It is much easier to make improvements when the original has paved the way.

The movie begins with publishing mogul and playboy David Aames (Tom Cruise) awakening to his voice alarm with the words continually repeated, "Open your eyes." The voice is that of Sofia (Penelope Cruz) who has not yet even been introduced to David.

David arises, gets dressed, drives to work, and finds himself in a deserted Time's Square without people or traffic. He abandons his car, runs down the empty street, and wakes up next to his bed-buddy Julie (Cameron Diaz) whom he likes physically, but not romantically. It is now her voice on the voice alarm telling him to wake up.

Later, David is having a birthday party. He meets Sofia and the two are immediately enamored with one another. Julie shows up, uninvited, and jealously makes her presence known. David and Sofia spend the night together in platonic rapture. In the morning David leaves Sofia's apartment and finds Julie waiting outside. She's stalking him. In her jealousy she seduces David into riding in her car for a daytime tryst. In that moment David's entire life changes.

Julie is furious at being tossed aside and attempts a double suicide by driving off a bridge at eighty miles per hour. She dies, but David is only disfigured. He is no longer the handsome playboy a.k.a. "citizen dildo." He even resorts to wearing a mask to hide his deformity.

The movie now begins to fragment and splinter into alternate possibilities. In one alternative, David has reconstructive surgery and becomes whole again. He romances Sofia, and their whole future is before them. In another alternative, David loses Sofia to his best friend. He is still disfigured. People look at him as pathetic. He's a pitiful alcoholic who collapses in the gutter. In another alternative, Julie never died in the car accident. The two are still bed-buddies, and David beats her in a fit of incomprehension. In a fourth alternative, he is in jail for killing Sofia, although he thought he was killing Julie. A fifth alternative is that this is all an intricate frame-up by members of his board. They are trying to gain control of the corporation by driving him insane. And it may be working.

David is currently in jail telling this fantastic story to the prison psychiatrist, McCabe (Kurt Russell). David has no idea which version is real, what is dream and what is reality. He begins doubting his sanity. But then a strange figure occasionally enters his world and tells him, "You must overcome your fears and regain control. Take a hold of your life again, David."

It eventually turns out that this stranger is from yet a sixth alternative version of reality. Supposedly, this is the reality which is true. David was in a car crash. Julie died. David was disfigured. Despondent over his life, David commits suicide. But he was so rich, he had a contract with the cryogenic corporation, Life Extension. They froze his body and kept his brain functioning in a dream state. David had chosen the "Lucid Dream" option in which he could live a life in whatever manner he desired. However, things went awry when his dream became a nightmare and he lost all control.

The program has now been fixed, and David can go back to dream his life in whatever manner he chooses. He can live forever with Sofia in paradise. He is, after all, frozen in stasis. Or, if he so desires, he can return to normal reality. His disfigurement and injuries can now be repaired. It's been 150 years and medical technology has advanced. But it may be difficult to adjust. His finances won't last long. He will only live his normal life span. And Sofia has long since died.

Faced with an eternity of happiness with Sofia in a dream paradise, or returning to normal life, David chooses the latter. "I want to live a real life. I don't want to dream any longer." However, he must prove his faith in order to fully awaken from the dream world. He must jump off the skyscraper (David has a phobia of heights). He does so, and when the nearly interminable fall ends, a voice says softly, "Open your eyes."

Vanilla Sky calls into question, not only reality, but how we deal with reality. Any of the versions could equally be real. Even the final explanation may not quite ring true. For like all infinite regresses, David could still be dreaming.

But whether dream or reality, David's soul is growing. He realizes the effect treating someone as an object can have.

> "Consequences, David. It's the little things," says Tech Support.
>
> "The little things. There's nothing bigger, is there?" responds David.

He realizes that what Sofia said the first night was true. "Every passing minute is another chance to turn it all around." And yet, strangely, most of David's fond memories of Sofia are imaginary. For they took place in the "lucid dream" scenario. His love for Sofia is based mostly upon a subconscious projection of an ideal. And yet it seems the most meaningful experience of his life.

Vanilla Sky also touches upon the "lucid dream" technique of Tibetan Buddhism. Their "yoga of dreams" stresses the control of awareness during dreams. One strives to realize, while asleep, that one is dreaming. Perhaps this can carry over so that one realizes one is dreaming in waking life. Perhaps

David is dead and dreaming in the afterlife. Perhaps he only dreamt that he was frozen and is about to wake up. Perhaps this is the only way his mind can rationalize and accept the survival of consciousness after death.

SEVENTH ALTERNATIVE

CHAPTER SEVEN

MEMORY & IDENTITY

Who are we, if we can't remember our past? If fragments of time are missing, are we not, ourselves, also fragmented—and missing? Memory consolidation is thus crucial to building an identity and a soul. Its impairment results in an individual somehow lacking. Memory can thus be seen to mediate the structure of one's ego and inner self. It is a vital component of who we are. For one's spiritual essence can only have meaning if it can be remembered.

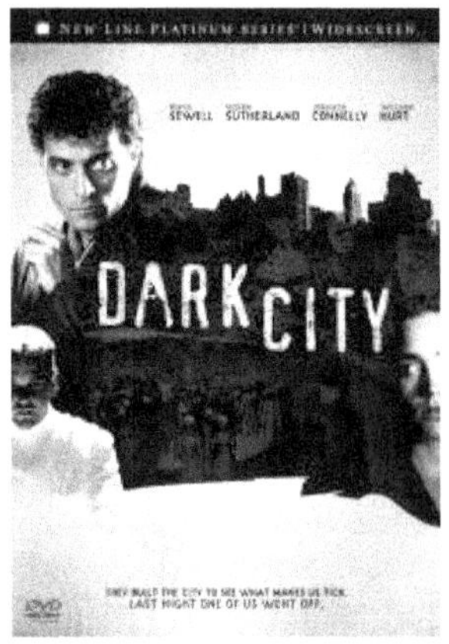

DARK CITY

Director: Alex Proyas
Producer: Alex Proyas & Andrew Mason
Screenplay: Alex Proyas, Lem Dobbs, &
David S. Goyer
1997 Color

How much of our soul and identity is determined by memory? If we forget our past, will we become a different person? Or will we become essentially the same person? Are memories what make us individual and unique? Or is it something else? The aliens in Dark City want to find out.

Director Alex Proyas and writers Lem Dobbs and David Goyer take us on a detective thriller gone awry. Awry, because it is intertwined in an alien experiment to find the human soul: a study of memory's place in determining who we are.

The movie begins with John Murdoch (Rufus Sewell) awakening in a hotel room. A murdered woman lies in a pool of blood on the floor. Was he responsible? He doesn't know, because he can't remember a thing. Even his name is revealed only by finding his wallet.

There have been a half dozen murdered women in "Dark City," and now John is the prime suspect. A telephone call warns him that people are hot on his trail. John flees the building, and continues fleeing throughout the movie. He flees from the police, and he flees from the aliens. For it just so happens that John is different.

John cannot sleep. When the clock strikes twelve, the entire city shuts down. People collapse and drift off to sleep wherever they happen to be. The city is then rearranged to suit the new environment of selected individuals whose memories are erased and replaced with the memories of others. The aliens have mastered the technique of distilling one's memories and injecting them into other people. "They think they can find the human soul if they understand how our memories work." The aliens, themselves, only have a collective memory, and now their civilization is dying. They need to understand human individuality in order to give new life to their race.

Is it memory alone that makes us unique?—or is there something more—a spirit or soul? "Will a man given the history of a killer continue in that vein. Or are we, in fact, more than the mere sum of our memories?"

John passes the test. Inside the apartment he had slipped and knocked over a goldfish bowl. He then picked up the floundering fish and released it in the bathtub. As the police detective observes: "What kind of killer, do you think, stops to save a dying fish?" A man who just committed a heinous murder would not care about a fish. Memories alone don't make us who we are, although they certainly are an essential ingredient.

John realizes something is amiss, not just his memory. There are strange, dark-cloaked figures that seem intent on killing or capturing him. John witnesses the spontaneous regeneration of the city: buildings shoot up into the sky while others move aside and expand. John realizes that he, too, can reshape the material world with an effort of will that the aliens call "tuning." He can make doors appear in blank walls, and then make them vanish after he passes through.

With the help of a human scientist (Kiefer Sutherland) who is being forced to aid the aliens, John is able to overcome their mind-control and fight them on a psychic level. He destroys the aliens and takes control of "Dark City" which turns out to be a drifting space platform or vessel. It doesn't matter what it is, because John can transform matter into anything he wants. He becomes the god of the new world, creates daylight and oceans. People will be allowed to live without their memories being constantly altered.

But who were they originally, and who are they now? John's wife (Jennifer Connelly) was previously a night-club singer. Now she is merely a ticket-seller at an old-time movie house. Who are we when our memories and lives have been so drastically manipulated?

At least for now, people can live in peace while forming new memories. They have a stable foundation upon which to build their lives. But what of the aliens' original question? Are we just memories, or is there something more?

John answered their question all too well. We are something more. He saved the goldfish and resisted the new memories of being a murderer. John did have a unique individual soul. His soul was so powerful that he resisted the twelve o'clock sleep. He could also tap the "tuning" power of the shape-shifting machines. And so the aliens wanted to use John for their own purposes. His powerful human soul could help govern their society, keeping it fresh and alive.

But what made John's soul so valuable was, ironically, the very downfall of the aliens. He was unique and individual, and so he would not allow himself to become one with their collective. John was also on a higher level of consciousness. He was powerful, too powerful to submit to being controlled.

While Dark City does have its drawbacks in plot development, its initial premise is philosophically profound. Although memories do lay the foundation for personality and identity, the human soul remains unique and unassailable.

SUTURE

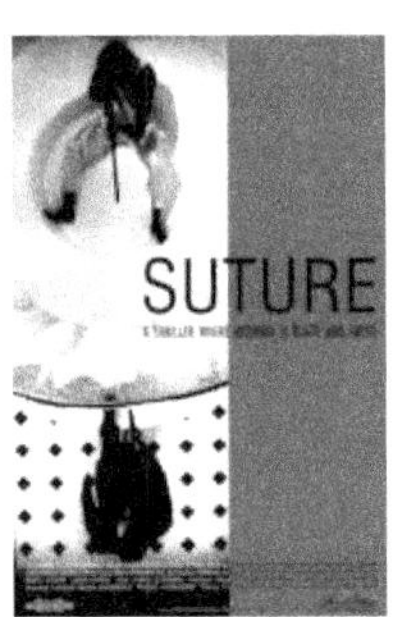

Director: Scott McGehee & David Siegel
Producer: Scott McGehee & David Siegel
Screenplay: Scott McGehee & David Siegel
1993 B & W

Memory is linked intricately to one's sense of self and individual identity. But is it also the essence of one's immortal soul? Directors/writers Scott McGehee and David Siegel tell the story of a criminal switch of identities, facilitated by one person's temporary amnesia.

The movie begins after the funeral of the father of two estranged half- brothers. The father and his son Vincent (Michael Harris) are extremely wealthy and powerful. The disowned and publicly-unacknowledged son, Clay (Dennis Haysbert), is an unsophisticated construction worker living in a poor, rural town. The two sons couldn't be more different. Clay is kind and gentle. Vincent is ruthless and cunning. In fact, the police suspect him of murdering his father and shooting an old woman eyewitness. A police line-up is scheduled, but until then Vincent is not officially charged.

Perhaps the most drastic difference between Vincent and Clay is that Vincent is slim and white, while Clay is black and husky with all the Negroid features of kinky hair and wide nostrils. However, everyone, including the brothers, believe they look uncannily similar—just like twins. This incongruity would seem to be tongue-in-cheek if not for the fact that it is the only discrepancy in the movie. Some symbolic commentary or social criticism seems apropos: perhaps how the world judges mostly by appearance. By the way, the movie is shot entirely in black and white.

The story continues with Vincent leaving overnight on an unavoidable trip. Clay drives him to the airport and will await his return. However, Vincent has dressed Clay in his own identical suit, and switched driver's licenses and credit cards. He has also planted a bomb in the car and detonates it while Clay drives the expensive car back home.

Vincent is fleeing to Mexico to avoid prosecution, while Clay lies seriously injured and burned, but not dead. He was thrown clear of the blast because he wasn't wearing his seat belt.

The ruse works to some extent. The authorities believe Clay is Vincent. The surgeons even reconstruct his face from photos so that he supposedly looks identical. What hampers the investigation and prosecution is that Clay has amnesia. He doesn't know who he really is, and merely accepts as fact that he is Vincent. However, his personality is still that of Clay: kind and gentle.

Clay strikes up a romance with his plastic surgeon, Renée (Mel Harris), a beautiful woman who can't believe Clay is guilty. The relationship develops to the point of marriage. Meanwhile, the police line-up has taken place. But the old woman says there is something different about Clay. Though extremely similar, she cannot testify for sure that he is the man who shot her and murdered his father.

Toward the end of the movie Clay's memory begins to return. He visits his home-town of Needles, California and begins to suspect his true identity. Meanwhile, Vincent has returned from Mexico intent on killing Clay for good. He enters his house in the dead of night, but Clay hears him and is waiting with a shotgun. Clay blows off Vincent's face and kills him. Now there is no proof of his real identity. It is simply a home invasion with justifiable self-defense, since Vincent was wielding a handgun.

Clay confesses to his psychiatrist everything that has happened. He reveals who he really is, but because of doctor-patient confidentiality, the psychiatrist cannot tell the police. Clay is bent on assuming Vincent's identity and forgoing his own past life. He has become settled in his new luxurious lifestyle. He doesn't want to become poor. He wants to marry Renée and live the life of the jet set.

The psychiatrist's voice-over ends the movie with shots of Clay's new life and wedding with Renée. The psychiatrist believes Clay has given up his soul, for the soul is inextricably bound to memory and identity. By forgoing his past memory and past life, Clay has traded away his true self. Just like Faust, he has sold his soul for power, women, and wealth.

Directors/writers Scott McGehee and David Siegel have created a simple plot to portray a modern-day Faust. Though unintentional and inadvertent, the mistaken identity was fully accepted. Even when both memory and identity were returned intact, Clay, the Faustian anti-hero, bargained his soul for a diabolical trade. Wouldn't all of us do the same?

LAST YEAR AT MARIENBAD

Director: Alain Resnais
Producer: Pierre Courau & Raymond Froment
Screenplay:Alain Robbe-Grillet
1961 B & W widescreen
French & Italian with English subtitles

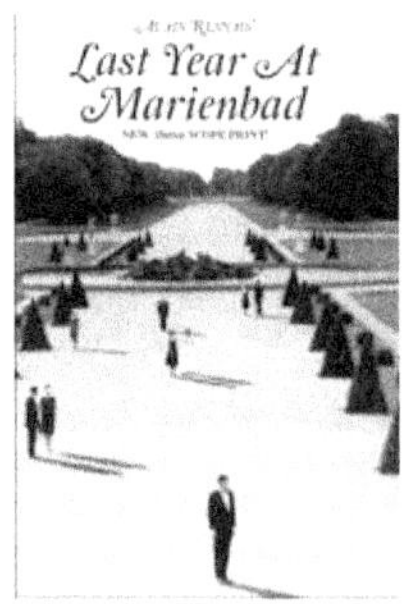

In Last Year at Marienbad, French novelist Alain Robbe-Grillet writes the film script for a primer on memory. This metaphysical construction is a thought-provoking exploration of the role memory plays in creating our subjective reality (which is the only reality we can ever really know).

The movie takes place in a luxurious resort-mansion. A man (Giorgio Albertazzi) meets a woman (Delphine Seyrig) whom he claims he met a year before at Marienbad? The woman is nonplussed and insists that he is mistaken. Could she have possibly forgotten? Doesn't she remember their brief affair? How she promised to meet him here one year later?

The woman denies the allegation. She believes the man to be mistaken in her identity. But as he becomes so much more excited and insistent, her fear turns to the possibility that he is dangerous or insane.

The man refuses to give in. Over and over he recalls in detail their actions at Marienbad. His relentless memories take her from gardens, through corridors, into salons, and lavish rooms. The camera follows faithfully. Is it an accurate rendition of the past? But wait—he is in error. He said they had met in the garden park. Now he remembers it was her room. "I can't remember exactly." Could he be confused? But the camera faithfully switches to the bedroom scene. Hence, the camera does not portray objective reality, but only the subjective reality of one's possibly flawed or possibly corrected memory.

And what of the woman's memory? At first she is so adamant that the man is mistaken, for she is and has been deeply involved with another man (husband or lover). But slowly the persuasive, almost hypnotic, re-telling of the past takes its toll. The mesmerizing tone of his voice and his total conviction, the continual repetition of scenes, down corridors into rooms, triggers some doubt.

As the man recounts their night of love-making, she hesitates and softens. She slowly walks backwards back to him. Then she becomes frightened and dashes away. Could it be true? Could she have forgotten—repressed her betrayal, her fling with another man? And now the emotions and feelings are overwhelming. She is filled with romantic passion for this stranger. Could what he says be true? His memories begin seducing her. But perhaps it is only fantasy? Perhaps her emotions and imagination have gone awry. Perhaps he has hypnotized her, conjured these images in her mind.

> "You asked me to allow you a year . . . to put me to the test, perhaps . . . or to weary me, or so that you could forget me. But time means nothing. I've come to find you."

The movie closes with an image of her response. They are together. She has left the other man. Were the images then real? Recovered lost memories?

That, in a nutshell, is the plot. The structure of the film is actually an exercise in remembering. But what's even more ingenious of Robbe-Grillet is that the physical setting, itself, is a portrayal of consciousness. The resort and its gardens are actually a symbolic embodiment of the structure of memory: a palace of memory—its marble walls and floors and balustrades, its marble statues frozen in action just as memory is frozen in time.

> " . . . forever, a past of marble . . . like this garden carved in stone . . . this mansion, its rooms deserted now . . . these still, silent, perhaps long-dead people . . ."

Because the past is over, it is as though frozen in time like marble. Even the people seem to be frozen in time, posed and stiff like mannequins and statues, only coming to life as the narrator remembers. And not only are people frozen as memories, but also what they are saying. Their very words are rigid—ossified by time. Their conversations are stiff and stilted—empty and lifeless—since they are only a memory of the past, waiting to be rescued by thought.

> "Conversation flowed in a void apparently meaningless . . . or, at any rate, not meant to mean anything."
> "A phrase hung in mid air, as though frozen . . . though doubtless taken up again later. No matter . . . the same conversations were always repeated . . . by the same colorless voices."

And now, for the last act of genius, Robbe-Grillet's thematic structure is itself a construct of memory. The self-conscious, self-reflective theme is apparent from the beginning. The people at the resort are attending a play which is a dramatization and encapsulation of the movie we are about to see—a Shakespearean play within a play. And just like a play or story—a memory is about something past, something already over, something that cannot be changed, cannot hope to be changed.

> "No, this hope is now pointless. Gone now this fear of losing such a link, a prison, a lie. This story is already over. A few seconds more . . . it has become frozen . . ."

> "The story is already over. A few seconds more, and it will finally be frozen . . . for ever, a past in marble . . . like the garden carved in stone . . . this mansion, its rooms deserted now."

And finally, for the masterful denouement, Robbe-Grillet ends the film with the narrator's puzzling admission. When you would expect happiness from the newly-reunited couple, instead, they seem resigned; their actions slow and deliberate, almost predestined—almost a memory. They seem lifeless, dead, just as the past is dead. The final shot is of the palace grounds.

> "The grounds of that mansion . . . were rather in the French style . . . without trees, flowers, or any plants. Gravel, stone, marble . . . rectilinear, formal, devoid of mystery. At first glance it seemed impossible . . . to get lost in them . . . along straight paths, between immutable statues . . . granite slabs . . . where you were, even now . . . losing yourself for ever in the still night . . . alone with me."

The man and woman are together, and yet alone, trapped forever in the maze of memories that are the constructs of life. For it seems that all our lives are just a memory. And all that matters is what we choose to remember.

Last Year at Marienbad is Robbe-Grillet's ingenious portrayal of how memory constructs reality. For if the past is forgotten, it may as well have never been. It is only by continual remembering that we know who we are.

> "No. I don't remember any more. I don't remember any more myself. I don't remember."

ETERNAL SUNSHINE OF THE SPOTLESS MIND

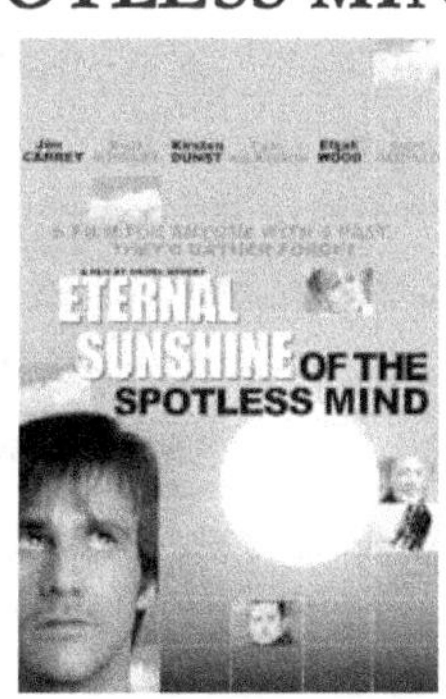

Director: Michel Gondry
Producer: Steve Golin & Anthony Bregman
Screenplay: Charlie Kaufman
From the story by Charlie Kaufman,
Michel Gondry & Pierre Bismuth
2004 Color

Memory is everything—to being human, to being alive. For what are we, if we can't remember? Our experiences constitute what makes up our lives. Without the ability to remember, we lose part of our souls.

In Eternal Sunshine of the Spotless Mind, director Michel Gondry and writers Charlie Kaufman and Pierre Bismuth illustrate the vital role memory plays in making us who we are. The movie is a romantic comedy with a science-fiction plot-twist. In a lighthearted manner it succeeds in conveying the inestimable metaphysical value of memory.

The movie begins with Joel (Jim Carey) impulsively ditching his day of work and taking a train out to the seashore at Montauk. He's not sure why, but it somehow seems important. Once there, he wanders the sandy beach as he writes and draws in his journal.

On the beach, in a coffee shop, and on the way back to the city, Joel keeps encountering Clementine (Kate Winslet), a strangely open, aggressive, and attractive young woman. At first he is put off by her annoying banter, but eventually her zany personality grows on him. He drives her home from the station and they have a friendly drink in her apartment. They seem to be mutually attracted, and Joel calls her for a date. They picnic the next night on the frozen Charles River, lying romantically side by side gazing up at the stars. They are up the whole night. In the morning Joel drives Clementine home, but she wants to go to sleep at his apartment. This is the prologue. The main body of the movie takes place in what turns out to be the past.

Joel and Clementine form a fun-loving, delightful couple. But eventually their differences begin to grate on each other. Like most spontaneous romances, the magic begins to wear off. They argue when Joel grows suspicious and insulting. Clementine impulsively decides to break it off.

The science-fiction element now enters. Lacuna, a medical brain-treatment facility, has the ability to eradicate selective memories. Clementine undergoes the procedure so she can wipe all traces of Joel from her mind. It is less painful that way. She can wipe the plate clean and start fresh with a new beginning. When Joel meets her at her bookstore, she treats him politely just like any other customer. She doesn't even know him. She doesn't remember.

Joel is tormented by her eradication of him. To get even, and to relieve his own anguish, he decides to do the same. The treatment takes place overnight in his own apartment. One by one each memory of Clementine is erased while he sleeps and dreams.

Joel slowly begins feeling regret. As their beautiful moments together are purged forever, Joel becomes panic-stricken. He changes his mind. He doesn't want to forget. In an hilarious attempt to hold on to the memories of Clementine, Joel tries hiding them in parts of his mind where they won't be discovered. Childhood scenes when he was four years old are re-enacted with Clementine. She, or her memory, becomes complicit in trying to evade the memory-wipe. Yet all to no avail. One by one each precious moment of life with her is expunged.

The special effects of the movie are metaphysically intriguing. Banks of light flash out one by one as the memory of an event dissolves. People in a crowd suddenly vanish as they pop out of existence. Buildings crumble and disappear as Joel's memory erodes. Backgrounds bleach white as he forgets.

In the final treatment scene, Clementine tells Joel this is it, this is her last memory. After this is gone, it will all be over. She will cease to have any existence in his life. In a last-ditch attempt to salvage their love, she tells Joel to meet her at Montauk.

Suddenly the viewer is catapulted to the future where the two meet (again) at the beginning of the movie. The secret assignation was successful (though how the real Clementine knew to meet in Montauk remains a mystery. Perhaps it was simply chance, or the forces of destiny.)

In any case, the two meet and uncover what had happened. A disgruntled employee (Kirsten Dunst) of Lacuna, who also had her memory wiped, believes the procedure to be a violation of human dignity. She sends tapes and files of every patient back to their unwitting owners. They'll be forced to come to terms with what they tried to forget.

Joel and Clementine are at first incensed by the situation. But then, as with all true love, they decide to give romance a second chance. Learning from the wisdom of what they tried to forget, perhaps they will avoid the folly of repetition.

Director Michel Gondry and writers Charlie Kaufman and Pierre Bismuth have created a humorous look at the importance of human memory. Eternal Sunshine of the Spotless Mind is a creative and playful portrayal of a very tragic and all-too-common problem. Alzheimer's and other neurological afflictions can cause memory-loss so severe that family members are not recognized. Imagine having to be told that the stranger greeting you is your own son. And how sad it is for others close to you. One of the joys of growing old is sharing memories of life together with your partner. How empty it must feel for the partner, when you don't even know you were ever married, much less to them.

Memories are golden. They are the sum total of life experience. Good or bad, they are who we are. To forget, is to diminish. To remember, is to learn and cherish. Eternal Sunshine of the Spotless Mind poignantly illustrates how memories are not only precious, but essential. For they are the building blocks of love, romance, and all human relationship.

AFTER LIFE

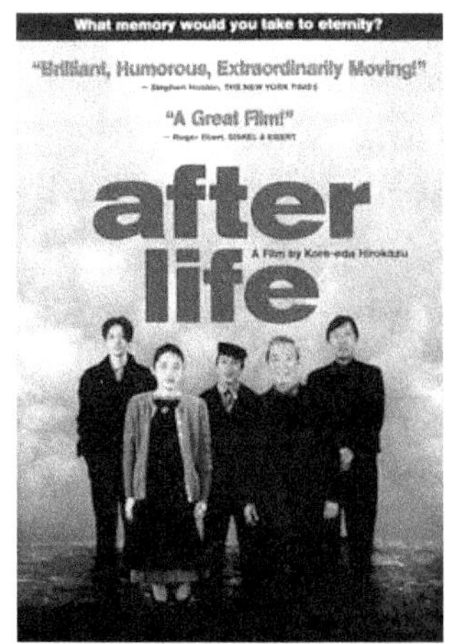

Director: Hirokazu Kore-eda
Producer: Shiho Sato & Masayuki Akieda
Screenplay: Hirokazu Kore-eda
1998 Color
Japanese with English subtitles

What happens when we die? Wouldn't we all like to know? If an afterlife exists, what would it be like? Who would we be? What would we remember?

In After Life, director/writer Hirokazu Kore-eda proposes an other-worldly existence with a gimmick. We can have only one memory of a past incident to live with and cherish forever! Eternity reliving one event from our former lives. All else will be forgotten. The results are a profound reflection upon the meaning of life. One must come to terms with values. One must settle accounts with one's soul.

The movie begins with the newly deceased arriving through the heavenly-lit doorway of a drab warehouse. They are assigned numbers and case-handlers who will assist them with their choice of a memory. The handlers will answer any questions, give any advice. If stymied in their choice, the departed may review film footage of their lives. They have three days to make a decision.

What memory would you live with? One of happiness and joy? One of love and tenderness? One of sexual ecstasy? One of meaning and profundity? One of religious awe or spiritual bliss? Remember, the deceased are limited to actual memories from their own lives. No fabrication is possible, for the heavenly assistants will see through it all. Only truth reigns in the afterlife. Lies and pretense are a thing of the past.

The newly departed make choices, but as the deadline draws near, some change their minds. A young girl picks her memory of Disneyland. "Lots of kids choose it," says Shiori, a young woman assistant-handler. "Especially teenage girls." The offhand comment makes the girl reflect. Does she want childish bliss or something more? In the end she decides on something more. She chooses a memory of resting her head in her mother's lap when she was three years old—a far more personal and spiritual choice.

Another man goes on and on about sexual pleasure and about how many women he's had. That will be his choice: carnal ecstasy is what it's all about. "Ask anyone," he remarks confidently. But as the deadline approaches, he changes his mind. He chooses instead his daughter's wedding when she's handing her parents the bouquet.

An unusual case is that of a somewhat unresponsive, old woman of around seventy or eighty. She seems childlike and autistic. Perhaps she is senile. It is finally discovered that she had chosen her memory long ago. She'd been living that memory of a nine-year-old girl for many years.

Two people out of twenty-two have problems making a decision. The deadline is approaching and one can't choose at all. He is seventy-year-old Watanabe (Naito Taketoshi). He needs something to jog his memory, and so tapes of his life are brought in for review. After days of watching videos he finally makes his choice: a day in the park when he and his wife of forty years agreed to start going to the movies once a month. Unbeknownst to him, his life and his choice are intertwined with that of his young handler, Mochizuki (Arata).

Before she knew Watanabe, his future wife had been in love with and engaged to a young soldier. He had shipped off during World War II and been fatally wounded. She continued to love him, and each year placed flowers on his grave. That young soldier is Mochizuki, Watanabe's handler. He appears young only because he died when he was twenty-two. Mochizuki keeps it all to himself, because the situation is too painful.

A further complication is the status of the handlers. They are also the departed who could not choose a memory. They must remain in limbo, processing others until they themselves arrive at a choice. Perhaps helping others will give them new insight. In Mochizuki's case, it does. He reviews the chosen memory of his beloved fiancee who had passed five years ago. It is the day in the park when he left to go fight in the war. It is the same park, possibly even the same bench as Watanabe's.

Mochizuki's choice is becoming clearer, but it is complicated by another factor.

The young woman assistant-handler, Shiori, has fallen in love with him. If he chooses a memory of his fiancee from the past, it will be as though she herself never existed. She will be wiped forever from his mind and soul, since their friendship only started in the limbo of the afterlife.

And now for a "departure" before returning to Mochizuki's dilemma. The other case of non-choice involves Iseya, a young, rebellious man of twenty-one who refuses, outright, to choose: "I have no intention of choosing. None." Day after day he stubbornly resists. He explains to Watanabe the reason for his unreasonable attitude: "For me, it's not that I can't. It's that I won't. I won't choose. You see, I decided this is the way to take responsibility for my life." By choosing only one memory he will blot out his entire existence. By not choosing, all his memories and actions will remain: something for him to ponder and reflect upon for all eternity.

The young rebel's rebellion influences Mochizuki's own decision. He knows what he must do. He chooses a memory from the afterlife of himself sitting alone on the same park bench, reflecting over his entire life. He will be able to keep it all—even his memory of Shiori and of his job in the afterlife. The supervisor of the handlers says: "We'll make a special exception in your case. Congratulations."

The movie ends with Mochizuki passing on to the next level, and Shiori taking his place as the new handler. Iseya, the young rebel, now takes Shiori's place as the new assistant-handler. Mochizuki's last words are haunting, for they come from the depths of his struggling soul. "All the time, I searched desperately inside myself, for any memory of happiness. Now, fifty years later, I've learned I was part of someone else's happiness. What a wonderful discovery." For someone he loved had chosen an eternal memory of him.

After Life is a profound reflection upon the meaning of life and of one's memories. Director Hirokazu Kore-eda has created his own vision of unearthly paradise—a heavenly realm where a single memory dominates and reigns supreme.

CHAPTER EIGHT

DAMAGED BRAINS

How important a role does the brain play in spiritual matters? The mental organ is purely physical. And yet its impairment results in debilitating consequences. Although distasteful to spiritualists, the physical organ plays an immense role in mediating one's metaphysical essence. Whether through disease, injury, or genetic mutation, afflictions of the brain deeply affect who we are; who we can become; and how we perceive the reality of our lives.

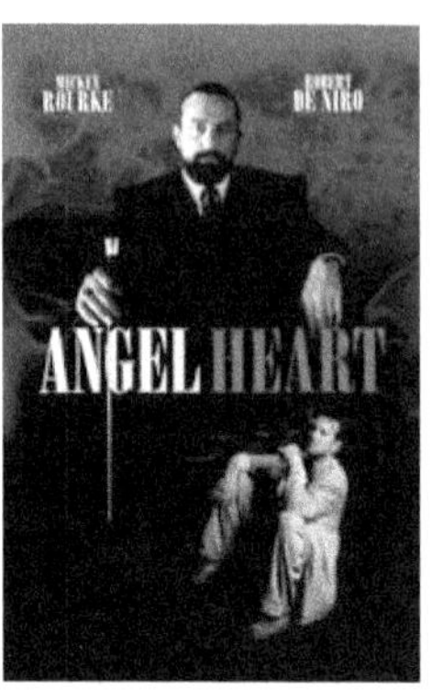

ANGEL HEART

Director: Alan Parker
Producer: Alan Marshall & Elliot Kastner
Screenplay: Alan Parker
Based on the novel Falling Angel by William Hjortsberg
1987 Color

Angel Heart is a detective thriller in which the object of the hunt is one's memory and soul. Director Alan Parker begins the film with a seemingly innocuous and routine investigation. Harold Angel (Mickey Rourke) is a private eye whose skills are enlisted by a client, Mr. Louis Cyphre (played by Robert De Niro).

Harold is to track down a man from Louis Cyphre's past— a certain Johnny Favorite, a big-band singer with whom Louis had a valuable contract. The problem is that during World War II Johnny became shell-shocked and had acute amnesia. He was then taken from a sanatorium under suspicious circumstances, replete with bribes and cover-ups.

Cyphre believes that, even now, Johnny may not remember who he is or was. The only way for the contract to be honored is for Harold to find Johnny so that Louis Cyphre can make him remember.

Harold finds the doctor, who treated Johnny, with his brains blown out. Harold wants out. Nothing was ever said about murder. But with sufficient monetary incentive, Louis Cyphre entices him to continue. But the bodies keep piling up. Witness after witness who knew Johnny, turn up dead, and always after Harold has just seen them. He thinks he's being set up and framed. But the truth is . . .

Harold himself is amnesiac. Or is it split personality? Or is it spirit possession? His investigation leads him from New York to New Orleans. He becomes immersed in both the backwater voodoo culture and the aristocracy of the Cajun south.

The clues slowly emerge. Johnny had been involved in a Satanic cult. He had sold his soul to the Devil in a Faustian pact for fame and fortune. After fame and fortune, Johnny wished to avoid paying the consequences. In a sacrificial ritual to trick the Devil, he murders a soldier look-alike, ripping out his heart and devouring it while it is still beating. He will acquire the soul of his victim and take his place. The Devil will be cheated from claiming Johnny's soul, since Johnny now has a different soul.

But complications arise. Before Johnny can drop out and re-surface as his victim, he is drafted, and during battle suffers from shell-shock. He is shipped home and institutionalized. His devilish cohorts in the ritual sacrifice try to complete the transformation. They pull the amnesiac Johnny from the sanatorium and dump him in Time's Square on New Year's Eve. For it was on New Year's Eve that they had abducted the soldier-victim and sacrificed him for their evil needs. Hopefully, Johnny will be transformed and thus escape paying the Devil his due. It works only too well. Johnny believes he is the person he killed—but he doesn't know that he is really Johnny.

Everything slowly begins to dawn on Harold Angel, the detective. He begins screaming hysterically as he hears the truth. He doesn't want to hear it. He knows it is true. Who was the soldier-victim? His dog tags were sealed in a vase. Harold finds the vase, smashes it, and pulls out the dog tags. The name gleams in shiny metal: Angel, Harold. Harold is the evil, devil-worshipper Johnny Favorite. It was he himself who had sadistically killed all five witnesses in an horrific manner.

The twelve-year search comes full circle. The memory lost is regained. Johnny had been hired to find himself. For Louis Cyphre ("Lucifer") is powerless to claim a soul, if the soul in question has no knowledge of the debt. If Johnny truly believes he is Harold (because he stole his soul and ate his heart), and was now amnesiac from shell-shock—then he was effectively untouchable. Only by remembering who he is, only by remembering his Faustian pact, can the Devil lay claim to Johnny's soul.

Director Alan Parker and novelist William Hjortsberg create a devilish movie about meaning and identity. Memory is the key to our sense of self, our identity. For without it we can never really know who we are.

"I know who I am!

I know who I am!

Satan!"

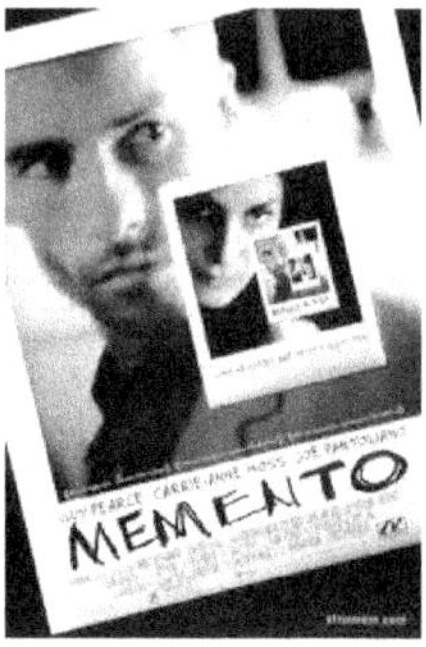

MEMENTO

Director: Christopher Nolan
Producer: Jennifer Todd & Suzanne Todd
Screenplay: Jonathan Nolan & Christopher Nolan
Based on the short story "Memento Mori" by Jonathan Nolan
2000 Color/B & W

"Memories can be distorted.

They're just an interpretation."

Memento is an ingenious thriller about how memory is necessary for the construction of both our identity and reality. Director Christopher Nolan takes us on a fragmented journey backward in time, uncovering piecemeal clues that will help us understand the present.

Leonard (Guy Pearce), the protagonist, is on a mission to avenge his wife's rape and murder. The interesting problem is that he has a bizarre mental condition. During the attack on his wife, he suffered a blow to the head. The brain injury was to the hippocampus, an area necessary for mediating short-term memory to long-term memory. The condition (anterograde amnesia—which people actually suffer from) results in the inability to form new memories.

Leonard remembers everything about himself and the world before the accident. But he is oblivious to everything after the accident. Everything that happens after his injury may as well not exist. For Leonard is trapped in the present moment. He cannot form lasting memories. His short-term memory lasts for only a few minutes, then he forgets. He forgets what started the conversation, the plot of the movie, who he had been talking to, where he is and where he was. All a person has to do is leave the room for ten minutes, and come back in, and Leonard won't remember that he knows them. He could have spent hours or days and weeks in their presence; could have slept with them; or saved their lives. It makes no difference, for they are only strangers. Jokes can be told to him a hundred times, and each time he'll laugh just as though it were the first. He can be insulted, beaten, and lied to—but the next time they can pretend to be his greatest friend. Leonard won't remember. He won't know the difference—unless . . .

Leonard makes post-it notes to catalogue his discoveries. The most important facts he has tattooed on his body. He takes polaroids and labels them with names and descriptions: "Teddy. Don't believe his lies."

But predictably, people use Leonard for their own ends. They can wrap him around their finger and manipulate him to commit crimes. Despite his efforts to organize, control, and make sense of his life, Leonard is lost in a maze of lies, half-truths, and facts—and he's not sure which is which. He is caught in a web of possible and contradictory interpretations.

"You don't have a clue, you freak.
You don't know what's going on . . .
You don't know who you are."

The action sequence of the film runs backwards in segments. The plot becomes clearer as it unravels toward the beginning. While people have used Leonard as a weapon against those they wish to exploit, it's his disability through which Leonard gets his revenge. All that's needed is a few words scribbled on a polaroid: "He is the one. Kill him." And when he awakens with no memory the new Leonard will believe the old.

Leonard uses his own mental condition to trick himself into getting the poetic justice he deserves. While others have used his mental disability to suit their own needs, Leonard now uses his disability to serve his own end. He knowingly uses his unknowing self.

What the Nolan brothers ingeniously portray in Memento is the vital role memory plays in constructing our subjective reality. And not only our reality, but also our identity—our sense of self. The real medical condition of anterograde amnesia wreaks havoc on people's lives. They are trapped in the present. They can read the same newspaper day after day for years, and yet each time it is new, it never grows old. Anterograde amnesiacs can never go forward in their lives, because they lack the memories necessary to weave continuity into their world. These memories form the basis from which to learn, build upon, progress and grow.

Memory is essential in forming a sense of identity or sense of self, because without it we could commit the most heinous acts of murder, and wake up the next day believing we are a boy scout or a saint.

> "That's who you were. You do not know who you are—what you've become since—the incident."

Indeed, by the end (or should I say "beginning") of the movie, Leonard has murdered three people. And yet he acts convincingly like an innocent, good-hearted victim. And, in his own mind, he is, because he simply can't remember. It is the oldest dodge in the book (from grand jury testimony to eye-witness intimidation). But in Leonard's case, it just happens to be true. For him, and those afflicted with anterograde amnesia: today is indeed the first day of the rest of your life.

> "I have to believe in a world outside my own mind. I have to believe that my actions still have meaning. Even if I can't remember them."

THE MAN WITHOUT A PAST

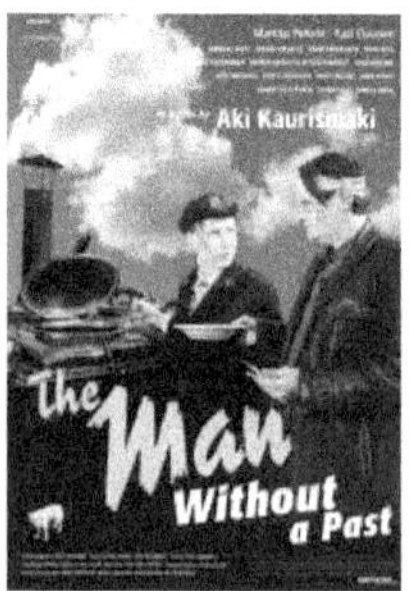

Director: Aki Kaurismäki
Producer: Aki Kaurismäki
Screenplay: Aki Kaurismäki
2002 Color
Finnish with English subtitles

Sometimes losing one's memory may not be all that bad. Depending upon one's prior life, forgetting may be a blessing. In a sense, losing the past may mean having a second chance. Not many of us have the opportunity to begin again, to wipe the slate clean and start afresh.

In The Man Without a Past, writer/director Aki Kaurismäki explores the beneficial aspects of losing one's memory. The movie begins with a man (Markku Peltola) arriving by train in an unfamiliar city (Helsinki). He spends the night on a park bench, dozing beside his suitcase. Three thugs come upon him, and he is mugged without knowing it. While unconscious in his sleep, he is knocked unconscious (possibly for good). The man has been waylaid by a blindsided whack on the head from behind. He never knows what hit him before he's out cold. The hooligans have a field day, using his head and body as a kicking and punching bag. They ransack his possessions and leave him for dead. The problem is that they toss his wallet and identification in the trash.

The man regains consciousness and staggers back to the train station. He collapses in the lavatory and is presumed to be dead. But we next see him in a hospital bed. A doctor watches his pulse slow and his heartbeat flat-line. He then pronounces him dead, and the nurse covers him with a sheet. But suddenly, when the doctor and nurse are gone, the man regains consciousness(once again) and rises from his deathbed.

The man leaves the hospital and collapses on the shore near a shantytown made of shipping containers. An old man steals his boots while he is unconscious. Perhaps he, like all the others, takes him for dead. But two boys find the man and notice he is still moving. They fetch their father, and he is taken in and nursed back to good health by the mother.

The problem: "I don't even remember who I am." He is suffering from irreversible "retrograde" amnesia.

The poor family helps him get back on his feet. They find a place for him to stay (another unoccupied shipping container). They help him find his bearings in this strange, unpredictable city. The man is introduced to free meals hosted by The Salvation Army. He is given nice, used clothes and even provided with a low-paying job.

Things are looking brighter. The man becomes attracted to Irma (Kati Outinen), one of the Salvation Army ladies who has helped him the most. She, too, is attracted to the man, and so they begin to date and romance.

The man is growing happy, despite his loss of memory (or perhaps because of it). He is content with his simple, near-poverty lifestyle. He begins to make friends and even organizes the Salvation Army band to play more popular music.

Just when it seems he's on top of the world, fate intervenes. The man inadvertently witnesses a bank robbery. The police become suspicious about his "phony" loss of memory and identity. They think he may be involved in the robbery. His picture is flashed through the media asking for help in identification.

The police roll up to the man's shanty shack with supposedly good news. "Your name is Jaako Antero Lujanen. . . . You are a metal worker from Nurmes." His wife has positively identified him from the police photo.

Jaako and Irma must part. The romance is over before it has really begun. After all, he is now a married man. He must return to his God-sanctioned life. For Irma is, foremost, a Christian member of the Salvation Army. Obviously, it is the only thing to be done.

Jaako reluctantly leaves Irma and Helsinki, and travels north to his wife in Nurmes. However, he still remembers nothing from the past. His wife must tell him all about their married life. They weren't getting along. They fought constantly. They were in the process of getting a divorce.

When Jaako disappeared after going for a job down south, she figured he just ran off, that he no longer cared. Because she never heard from him, their divorce was approved and finalized. They are no longer married. She is now involved romantically with another man.

It's all the same to Jaako, because he doesn't even know her. She is a stranger to him, so why should he be jealous? His past is someone else's past. They part amicably, and Jaako returns south to Helsinki.

He finds Irma. She thought she had lost him forever. Now they can begin again, start life afresh. It turned out to the advantage of all. Sometimes losing the past is best for everyone.

Director/writer Aki Kaurismäki has created an interesting plot about memory-loss and second chances. Most movies about brain injuries and memory impairment depict the phenomena in a negative light—all the restrictions and disabilities that such injuries entail. But in The Man Without a Past, the victim is shown to have actually been graced by his blows. For his past had been eradicated. He could resume life as innocently as a newborn.

The psychological and metaphysical ramifications are profound. Memory is the substrate which identity builds upon. When the memory is wiped clean, there is no longer an identity. And yet there remains a conscious soul and personality. Such a soul can start afresh, building a new identity by creating newly-formed memories. Jaako will do just that, for he has been given a new life and a second chance. Maybe all of us could use a few blows to the head.

AWAKENINGS

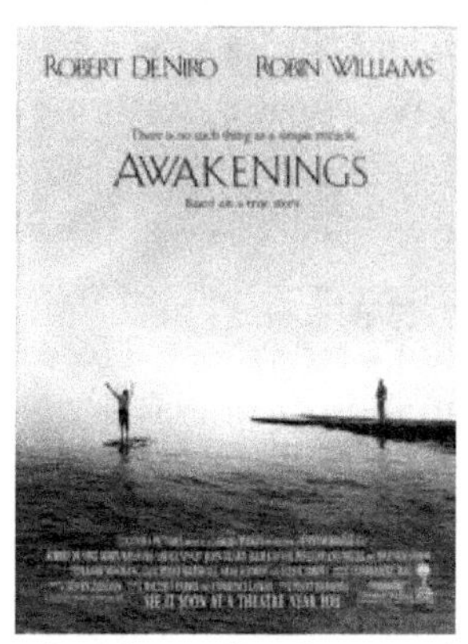

Director: Penny Marshall
Producer: Walter F. Parkes & Lawrence Lasker
Screenplay: Steven Zaillian
From the book by Oliver Sacks
1990 Color

How much in life do we take for granted? Taking a simple walk. Conversing with others. Shopping for food. Raising an arm. Scratching an itch. When we see a quadriplegic in a wheelchair, do we not say, "There, but for the grace of God, go I?" And then we go about life, taking everything for granted.

In Awakenings, director Penny Marshall and writers Oliver Sacks and Steven Zaillian portray the lives of fifteen catatonic patients who suddenly come to life. After a period of up to thirty years or more, a new drug therapy enables them to return to normal and literally "wake up." The amazing story is true. Well-known writer/neurologist Oliver Sacks (whose name in the movie is changed to Dr. Sayers) experimented with the drug L-dopa. The result was both a success and a failure. However, the movie brilliantly succeeds, conveying an appreciation for the simple act of being alive.

The story begins with Dr. Sayers (Robin Williams) accepting a position in a hospital for the treatment of neurological disorders. It isn't long before he takes interest in a group of catatonic patients whose common denominator is having contracted encephalitis lethargica (sleeping sickness) earlier in their lives. Sayers theorizes that their condition is due to progressive brain damage at an early age. He further links the encephalitis lethargica to Parkinson's disease for which the drug, L-dopa, is the current treatment.

With the approval of the hospital administration, and the consent of the patient's family, Dr. Sayers administers L-dopa to one patient, Leonard (Robert De Niro). At first there is no response. But as Sayers increases the dosage, there is a miraculous occurrence. Leonard awakens and is found sitting at a desk, writing in the middle of the night.

The hospital staff are amazed. With their help, Leonard gradually moves about and talks like a normal person. The recovery is spectacular. Leonard greets his mother for the first time in over thirty years. He was only a little boy when he was stricken with catatonia.

Dr. Sayers convinces the hospital administration to raise funds for the expensive L-dopa treatment. He wants all the catatonic patients who had been stricken with encephalitis lethargica to receive the same dosage. Once again the result is spectacular. The patients awaken after three decades of stupor and are ready to rumble. The ward is a bedlam of excitement. The patients go on field trips to regain some of the life that they've lost. They dance and party like never before.

Meanwhile, Leonard develops romantic feelings for one of the hospital visitors. Paula is visiting her father who had a stroke and is also catatonic and incapacitated. The problem with all the experimental patients is that up to thirty years of their lives are missing. They are stunted not only socially, but also psychologically. Leonard is really still just a young boy in a man's body. Another woman was a "flapper" from the twenties, and now she is an old woman in her fifties. What drastic psychological fallout for this miracle drug! But despite the treatment's repercussions, the patients can still begin to grow and adjust. After all, it is far better than being a catatonic zombie.

The psychological drawbacks of the L-dopa treatment turn out to be the least of its problems. After awhile the drug seems to be wearing off. Leonard begins to develop the tics and nervous condition of a Parkinson's patient. He also becomes "spacey" as he drifts in and out of trance. The effect of the drug seems to be reversing. Whether through habituation or some other reason, the chemical-window for L-dopa is closing. Leonard, and all the other patients, revert to their former catatonic condition.

The situation is a human tragedy. The ward had been filled with living, feeling, ecstatic patients; and now they are once again becoming zombies. Leonard tells Paula that this is the last time he will see her. He is jerking about and spasming uncontrollably as he rises to leave. "I'm grotesque," he had admitted in anguish to Dr. Sayers. Paula is stunned by the transformation. But she retains enough dignity and compassion to take Leonard in her arms and dance around the cafeteria floor. What grace and humanity some people possess!

The summer of 1969 was both a miracle and a tragedy. For human beings to awaken and live joyously, and then to be once again locked away inside their physically catatonic shells. What is truly horrible is that this story is factual. The encephalitis lethargica outbreak of the early twenties claimed thousands of souls. Perhaps what has been learned about the brain and the neurological disorder will save future victims from a similar fate. New drugs are developed continuously. Brain research progressively reveals more about the human mind.

Director Penny Marshall and writer/neurologist Oliver Sacks have created an amazing story of what it means to be human. We take so much for granted. To live. To speak. To write. To walk about and do simple chores. "People don't appreciate the simple things: work, play, friendship, family." Life itself is the miracle. Being human and interacting with others is the blessing. For there, but for the grace of God . . .

THE MIRACLE WORKER

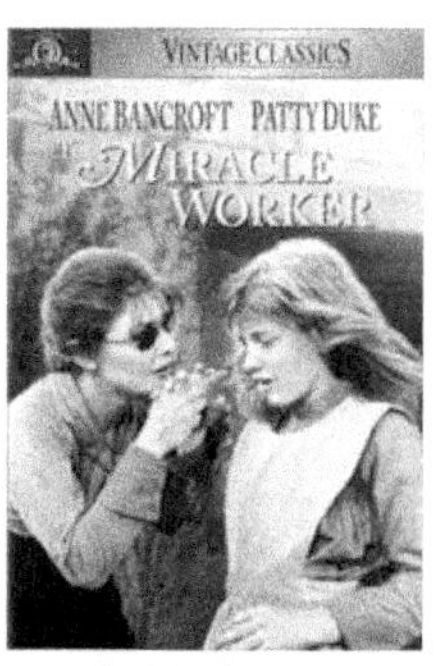

Director: Arthur Penn
Producer: Fred Coe
Screenplay by William Gibson
from his play The Miracle Worker
1962 B & W

Of all the real-life stories that movies have portrayed, none can be more inspiring than The Miracle Worker. Based upon the life of Helen Keller, the film depicts the transformation of a blind, deaf-mute into a fully "self-actualized" human being. Her accomplishments, the obstacles she surmounted, make the average person's life a shameful embarrassment. For we do so little, we have it so easy. And yet a severely handicapped woman can write books, give lectures, learn four different languages, graduate with honors from Radcliffe College, and lastly, be awarded the Presidential Medal of Freedom: the highest award possible for an American civilian.

The movie begins with the arrival of Anne Sullivan (Ann Bancroft)—a novice teacher who becomes a stern disciplinarian. She realizes that Helen's family is too indulgent. They let Helen (Patty Duke) grab food off their plates, stuffing it in her mouth with her bare hands. She is allowed to throw tantrums, run wild, and have her way with everything. And they are always supportive, as if she were a perfect child.

Anne realizes that Helen will never learn if the family gives in to their pity and compassion. They are condemning Helen to a life of uncontrollable self-indulgence, the life of an animal, or at best that of a pet. And so Anne begins a regimen of discipline that tames the "wild beast." And once Helen is tamed she gradually becomes receptive to learning.

Anne begins teaching American Sign Language to Helen. For most of the film, Helen only communicates in a sort of stimulus-response type of interaction. She does not really "know" what she is "saying." From their studies of animal and inter-species communication, psychologists are aware of the problems of fully grasping a language. As some behaviorists maintain, sign language and symbol-manipulation experiments with great apes do not represent true communication in a language. They argue that even pigeons can memorize up to five or six colored balls that, when pecked at in the correct order, results in the stimulus-response reward of food or water. Does that mean the pigeon comprehends that it is asking, "You—give—pigeon—food—water." Or isn't it more likely that the dumb bird has simply memorized a sequence of colored pecks that will result in a reward?

Helen's case is similar. And Anne realizes that, though Helen knows the symbols, she doesn't yet grasp the intricacies of grammar, syntax, and true language. It is only at the movie's climactic ending that Helen fully comprehends the meaning of her finger-manipulations. Rather than a symbolic stimulus-response with no understanding, Helen now knows that those finger symbols are actually letters that spell words, and the words represent things—all sorts of things. Everything. The scene at the pump brings tears as Helen feebly vociferates "water" as a dawning light shines in her unseeing eyes.

Neurologists and anthropologists are fully aware of what is transpiring at the water-pump. For they know that language is what truly separates man from the beasts. Animals do have limited language capability. But fully elaborate language occurs only in humans. It has allowed one generation to pass on knowledge and skills to future generations. It has allowed one culture with a different language to interpret and then learn from another culture. It has allowed mankind to build upon itself—civilization after civilization. All that is truly great has been built upon language.

And so, Helen, a deaf, blind, mute not so different from a pet animal, suddenly breaks through the sound-barrier and begins to understand. The anthropological history of the human race is suddenly encapsulated in the enlightenment at the pump.

While Helen's achievements are immortalized in movies, plays, and books, there is a second heroine who must not be overlooked. Anne Sullivan was the real "Miracle Worker." Without her, Helen would be little more than an animal, probably cared for in a sanatorium. It was through Anne's diligence and "teachings" that Helen became the true human being she was always capable of becoming.

The playwright, William Gibson, must be credited for his acknowledgement of Anne. For his title, The Miracle Worker, places Anne Sullivan's role in proper prominence. One must not forget that this Miracle Worker, herself, was also handicapped. She too had been blind, and was still recovering from a recent sight-restoring surgery when she met Helen.

There is no greater bond between two human beings than language. Even love pales and is diminished if not expressed through words. What can possibly equal the gift of love, if not the gift of true language? Helen, herself, acknowledges the paramount importance of Anne's gift of language and love. In her autobiography she writes:

> The most important day I remember in all my life is the one on which my teacher, Anne Mansfield Sullivan, came to me. . . . I stretched out my hand as I supposed to my mother. Some one took it, and I was caught up and held close in the arms of her who had come to reveal all things to me, and, more than all things else, to love me.[1]

> . . . my teacher—who was to set my spirit free.[2]

In a world of trendy superstars, rock icons, and vain athletes, modern culture is bereft of meaningful heroes and heroines. Ann Bancroft lamented her legacy in an interview before her death in 2005:

> Why is it people remember me for being Mrs. Robinson (in The Graduate)? Why don't they remember me for my role as Anne Sullivan?
>
> (paraphrased—parenthesis mine)

In a society which eschews the concept of a "hero" as somehow childish, I reluctantly admitted to friends an addition to my shortlist of heroines: Helen Keller and Anne Sullivan.

---

1. Helen Keller, The Story of My Life (New York: W.W. Norton & Company, 2003), pp. 25-26.

2. Ibid., p. 16.

CHAPTER NINE

ACTS OF CREATION

Man was created in the image of the gods. And like the gods, he, too, aspires to create. Perhaps no other human activity is as meaningful as the act of creation. Whether it is an artist painting a canvas, an author writing a novel, a musician improvising or composing, or a scientist formulating a theory—creating culture makes us more than animals. It is what makes us human, and perhaps more than human. Perhaps it is the creative impulse that sets man on a par with the gods.

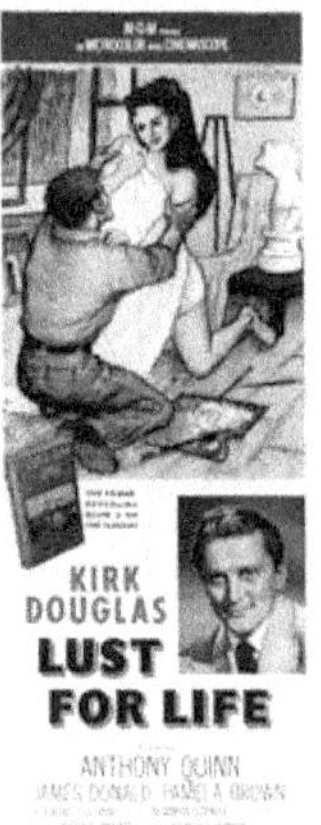

LUST FOR LIFE

Director: Vincente Minnelli
Producer: John Houseman
Screenplay: Norman Corwin
From the novel by Irving Stone
1956 Color

To create from the soul, however tortured that soul. Lust for Life is the story of the troubled Dutch artist Vincent van Gogh. Director Vincente Minnelli adapts the novel by Irving Stone, bringing to life the color of both Vincent and his art. His paintings now sell for millions. But while alive (out of over 1500 paintings and drawings), he sold only one. Unrecognized, a failure and misfit to many, so unstable that he sliced off his own ear—van Gogh is now considered a genius. His life was tragic, but it was a life filled with passion, a "Lust for Life" and all it may bring.

The movie begins with Vincent (Kirk Douglas) taking a lay preacher's position in the Borinage mining district of Belgium. At first, he hasn't found his true calling. He believes the life energy overwhelming him was meant to spread the word of God.

As a preacher, he gives and suffers until there is nothing left. His brother, Theo, takes him back home where he recovers and begins to paint. Vincent learns fast, and is eager to learn more. When he travels to Paris, he meets other world-class painters who stimulate his growing and developing art.

Eventually Vincent leaves Paris for the countryside of Arles in southern France. The natural color and light of the outdoors alters his palette and his paintings. He dreams of founding an artist colony, and Gauguin (Anthony Quinn) is his first choice. Vincent craves artistic stimulation, as well as friendship for his lonely soul. Gauguin provides the stimulation all too well. After an argument, Vincent chases down Gauguin with a razor, but then retreats back home and cuts off his own ear. Gauguin leaves after the breakdown and breakup. Theo arrives to rescue Vincent from himself. Vincent voluntarily commits himself to an asylum where he recuperates while continuing to paint. Eventually he is well enough to return to normal life. He stays with Dr. Gachet who watches out for him as he recovers. Vincent paints the village life and countryside of Auvers.

As time passes, Theo gets married and has a son whom he names "Vincent." Theo continues sending Vincent money and supplies while trying to sell his works. With Theo's new family, Vincent feels he has become a burden. He feels himself a failure and parasite. In one of his fits of depression and loneliness he shoots himself in the chest. His attempt at suicide is itself almost a failure. But he dies two days later with Theo at his bedside. As in many close relationships, Theo dies within six months. He is buried in Auvers beside his brother, his friend.

Director Vincente Minnelli and writer Irving Stone create a beautiful and moving drama about a beautiful and moving life. Van Gogh, a great artist far ahead of his time, needed time to be appreciated for the posthumous genius he was to become. He is now considered the most recognized artist of all time.

Mankind considers van Gogh a tragic artist, a great artist, but a sad, lonely, and unbalanced artist. Should he be pitied? Not in the least. Despite the final outcome, van Gogh filled the world with a vision of meaning and beauty. His life was intense, and emotional. He knew the lofty heights and the pits of despair. Strangely, to all suffering, starving artists, he is an inspiration. For no matter what society says while you're alive, a time may come when your work is not only accepted, but extolled.

Vincent's art is now immortal. But his fervent life, overflowing, simply could no longer be contained. Who are we, mere mortals, to pity and pass judgment on such a man?—a man who had shared so much of his vitality with the world, a man with such creative genius, so much "Lust for Life."

FAHRENHEIT 451

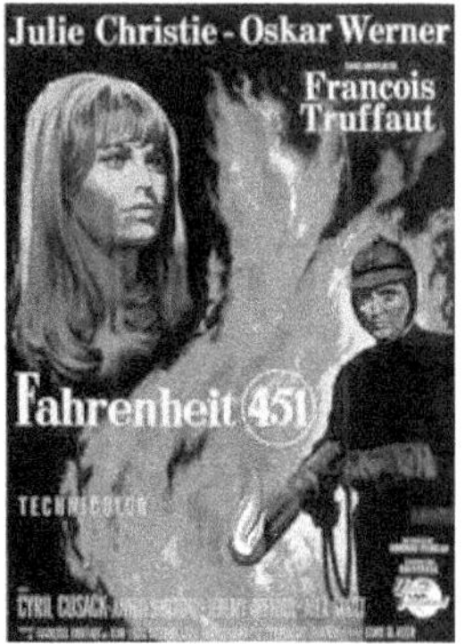

Director: Francois Truffaut
Producer: Lewis M. Allen
Screenplay: Francois Truffaut & Jean-Louis Richard
From the novel by Ray Bradbury
1966 Color

Perhaps the greatest stride in human evolution was the invention of language. Verbal words enabled communication between humans: passing on knowledge, skills, hopes and dreams across generations. But the next great stride was in developing written language. For writing endures, and can be deciphered by archaeologists removed in time by over six thousand years. The printed word marked a further stride, the true blossoming of human culture. For it was more or less permanent, almost eternal. And it could be mass-produced for the benefit of all society.

In Fahrenheit 451, director Francois Truffaut and writer Ray Bradbury tell the story of a future world where reading is forbidden and all books are banned. Those caught with books are punished. Firemen do not put out fires, they start them. They search out hidden book stashes and burn them in public—for the good of the community.

The totalitarian government is engaged in Orwellian thought-control. Books challenge authority, for they give people freedom of thought. But the government maintains that books are rubbish. They're dangerous because they make people unhappy and stir discontent. "Books disturb people. They make them anti-social." To enforce the ban, the authorities monitor everyone. Red information boxes with flashing blue lights allow for anonymous tips from informants. When a tip comes in, the firemen go out—raiding and vandalizing the outlaw-reader's residence. When they find an entire library, they simply burn down the house. They are even willing to burn those who stand in their way.

The movie's hero is Montag (Oskar Werner). Ironically he is a fireman, and more ironically he is the one (out of a nine-man crew) who operates the flamethrower that burns the books. For five years Montag has done his duty honorably and without question. He is on the verge of promotion when he meets Clarisse (Julie Christie), a school teacher who secretly (God forbid) likes to read. She questions Montag as to why he burns books. "Well, it's a job, like any other." But she persists, making him wonder as to the validity of the government's ban on books.

Montag begins to have doubts. His curiosity is aroused. He begins, clandestinely, to read some of the books he's supposed to have burnt. To his wife Linda (also Julie Christie), he is flirting with a dangerous obsession. She herself never questions authority, watches the government-run television programs all day, takes government-dispensed pills, and is generally a vapid housewife.

Montag and his wife are now on two different paths. He becomes intrigued by Clarisse, and the untold intellectual realm she has opened to his imagination. Montag is hooked. From a pyromaniac he has become a confirmed bibliomaniac. All he cares about is catching up on his stunted literary development.

To Montag's dismay, his wife and her friends can't be persuaded to his cause. He reads to them, but only one is affected by the words of a novel. She begins to cry. The others become defiant and claim that, "novels are sick." "Evil words that hurt people." It is the beginning of Montag's downfall. Where one would expect Linda's friends of being the informants—it is Linda herself who informs on her husband, leaving him to his fate.

On the last fire-run before Montag officially resigns, the fire truck stops in front of his own home. Montag falls victim to his wife's betrayal. He pulls out all his hidden library, and with a flamethrower, catches it afire. He also torches his bed and wall-screen television since his home-life is all but over. When the fire-chief pulls out Montag's favorite book, hidden in his jacket, Montag resists and points the flamethrower at the chief. The chief pulls his gun, and Montag ignites him in flames.

Montag is now wanted for murder. He is on the run from the authorities who are searching everywhere. Montag flees to the realm of the book-people who live deep in the woods. He arrives and is welcomed. Clarisse is there, as well as a host of other "books."

The book-people memorize their favorite books and then burn them so they can't be taken away. They keep to themselves, and so the government leaves them alone. They are, in effect, quarantined from infecting the rest of society.

In a beautiful and haunting climax to the movie, the outcasts wander through the forest; reciting their books to others; memorizing them for themselves; teaching the pages to the next generation of book-people. It is a book-lover's wonderland of literary characters who are, themselves, the veritable embodiment of the books they love. They constitute the surviving literature of mankind, an outdoor library of the human race.

Fahrenheit 451 dramatizes the value of the written word. Director Francois Truffaut and writer Ray Bradbury convey how precious and meaningful books are to humanity. They are the foundation for cultural and spiritual evolution. In a totalitarian police state with a mind-numb society, the book-people exemplify the radiant hope of man's spirit. "The secret they carry is the most precious secret in the world. With them, all human knowledge would pass away."

THE AGONY AND THE ECSTASY

Director: Carol Reed
Producer: Carol Reed
Screenplay: Philip Dunne
From the novel by Irving Stone
1966 Color

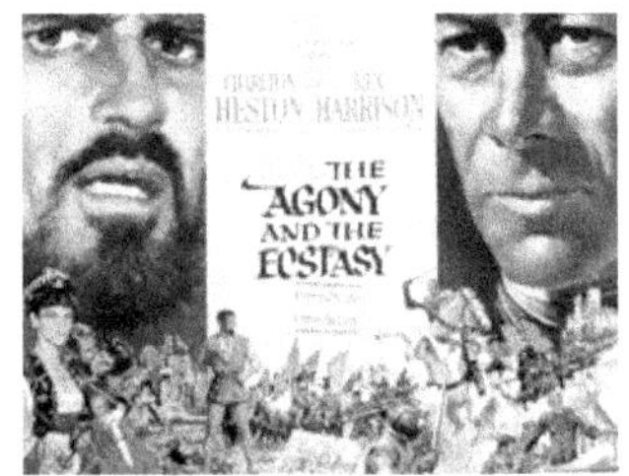

Creating a miracle. Being the instrument in the creation of something magnificent and divine. The result is so much greater, so much more sublime than the individual. The work of art becomes immortal, lasts for centuries, perhaps millennia. It inspires those who wish to reach beyond, stirring the hopes and dreams of mankind.

Director Carol Reed and writer Irving Stone portray the drama of Michelangelo's painting of the Sistine Chapel. Michelangelo (Charlton Heston) is a Florentine sculptor who works in marble. He doesn't want to paint, although a master. He only wants to sculpt.

Pope Julius II (Rex Harrison), his employer and patron, nevertheless has other plans. The Sistine Chapel needs improvement, something to make it truly grand. It is too plain for the papal Mass. He wants the ceiling painted in fresco to reflect the glory of God.

Michelangelo must abandon his present assignment of creating marble sculptures for the Pope's tomb. His spirit rebels, but his hands are tied. He must follow the wishes of the Pope.

Florentine fresco painters are hired as assistants to Michelangelo. The project begins along the lines the Pope has planned. But in a fit of discontent, Michelangelo destroys everything he has done. He flees Rome and hides out as a marble quarry-worker. The Pope hunts for him everywhere. Michelangelo flees into the mountains where he has a vision of what he should create. The inspiration brings him back to the Pope who is overcome by his enthusiasm.

Michelangelo now starts on his own vision of the Sistine Chapel. He dismisses the Florentine assistants because he wants to work alone. The project seems endless. Originally predicted to take months or a year at most, it instead takes years. "When will you make an end?" badgers the Pope repeatedly. "When I'm finished," replies Michelangelo defiantly each time.

As in any great endeavor, there are setbacks and personality clashes. Michelangelo is, at times, arrogant and insolent to the cardinals, and even to the Pope. He gets away with it for awhile, because he is recognized as an inspired genius. But eventually the tension mounts until the last straw falls. Michelangelo is struck by the Pope and dismissed.

The Pope is having problems of his own: wars, lack of funding, loss of political support. Michelangelo, himself, had a period where he felt he was going blind, and then became physically ill and discouraged. The Pope is also wounded in one of his campaigns to defend Rome. He falls seriously ill. At one point he is so weakened he is expected to die.

Michelangelo swallows his pride and humbly asks the Pope to reinstate his commission. The Pope agrees, and Michelangelo eagerly returns to work on the ceiling. After an interminable period, it is finally completed. The beauty and magnificence transcend anything the Pope could have imagined. He is humbled by what he sees on the ceiling of the Sistine. The vision is truly divine. "If I had to choose my life over again, I think I would choose to be an artist." He believes God is speaking through Michelangelo far better than through his position as the Pope. "You make a better priest than I do, Michelangelo."

All their differences and squabbles now seem ridiculous and petty. The Pope asks Michelangelo if he is now glad at being forced to paint the ceiling.

Michelangelo nods and adds humbly, “and grateful.” The Pope then adds, “I was moved by another hand as easily and skillfully as you move your brush.” Perhaps God acted through him in lending a small hand in Michelangelo’s creation.

Pope Julius II admits that his entire life will amount to very little in comparison to the Sistine Chapel. “I fear I shall be known not as the Pope who drove the invaders out of Italy, but one who forced an unwilling artist to complete his work—which is so much greater than both of us.” It will be his legacy, that he forced Michelangelo’s hand into painting an immortal work of art. The two are reconciled, and Michelangelo is allowed to return to work on his immortal sculptures.

Director Carol Reed and writer Irving Stone create their own masterpiece about the creation of a masterpiece. The spirit of a grand master, his vision and inspiration, all culminate in this moving portrait of the heavenly creation of man, and one man’s visionary creation of heaven. Man is so small, yet his vision can be so great. It is enough to make one believe in God.

AMADEUS

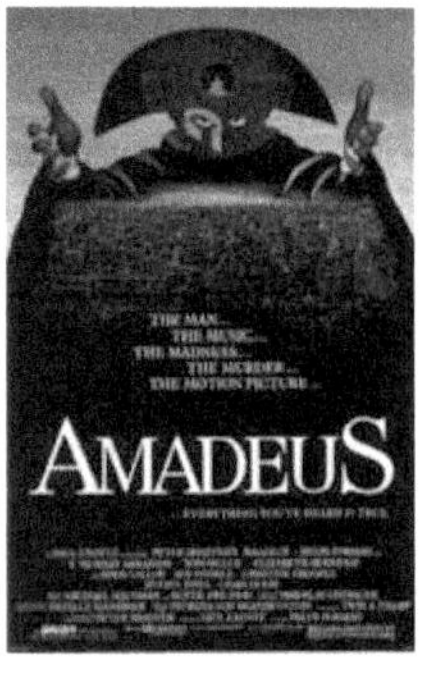

Director: Milos Forman
Producer: Saul Zaentz
Screenplay: Peter Shaffer
From the play by Peter Shaffer
1984 Color

What makes one man a genius, and another a mediocrity? Is it genes or environment that imbues one with creative talent—not just a dabbler’s ability, but rather a skill that marks the true master?

In Amadeus, director Milos Forman and writer Peter Shaffer pit the less-gifted Viennese court composer Antonio Salieri against the acknowledged genius of Wolfgang Amadeus Mozart (Tom Hulce). While the historical accuracy of the film is debatable, the immortality of Mozart’s music shines through the debacle which supposedly led to his death.

The movie begins with Salieri (F. Murray Abraham) attempting suicide and being taken to an asylum. A priest arrives to receive his confession, and to heal his troubled soul. Salieri relates his conflict with Mozart in flashbacks which comprise the structure of the movie.

Salieri has heard Mozart's work and admires him immensely. But when he meets him in person he finds a vulgar, carousing, boastful womanizer with an obscene giggle. What's more, Mozart upstages him continually—whether in rewriting and improving Salieri's own tribute to welcome Mozart to Vienna; or in mocking him at a costume ball where he ridicules Salieri's style and gestures.

Salieri, always strict and formal, is the complete opposite of playful, fun-loving Mozart. However, only Salieri realizes Mozart's true greatness. "It seemed to me I was hearing the voice of God." He curses God for allowing such talent to be contained within such a shameful facade. Whereas, he himself has been showered with mediocrity.

Salieri vows to work against God's design. He will thwart Mozart and God in every way, at every opportunity. His diabolical scheme is to work Mozart to the point of sickness and death.

Meanwhile, Mozart is producing incredible operas. But Salieri has used his influence to limit the number of performances just short of success. Mozart struggles financially. Finally, out of desperation he is forced to write operas for the vaudeville stage. "The Magic Flute" is the delightful result.

But Salieri has anonymously pressured Mozart for a death requiem. He has enticed him with bags of gold, if only it can be done quickly. Mozart works at a feverish pace. He is exhausted and ill-tempered. He snaps at his wife, then stays out partying all night. Frustrated, she leaves him to find refuge at a spa resort. She returns only in time to witness her husband pass away.

Salieri has his revenge on both Mozart and God. But he has destroyed one of the greatest musical prodigies the world has ever known. And thus, he attempts suicide, and is committed to an asylum. He is a bumbling failure even at his last, most serious act.

Amadeus is an inspirational comic-drama. Director Milos Forman and writer Peter Shaffer have given us a story that may very well be conjecture. Nevertheless, it still brilliantly illuminates the musical genius of Wolfgang Amadeus Mozart.

Why are some people endowed with such heavenly gifts while others languish in mediocrity? Perhaps the answer lies in the playfulness of imagination. Salieri was a stick-in-the-mud. Mozart was a passionate, exuberant, free spirit. His unlimited creativity may be due to his breaking the bonds of formality, convention, rules of discipline and order. By doing so, his genius may have transcended to an even greater order—the order of the gods . . . and of immortality.

CHAPTER TEN

THE MEANING OF DEATH

Death has the final word. It always has, and always will. But does death negate the meaning of life? If all our struggles simply end in decay; if the sinner shares the same fate as the saint, then what difference does it make? Why strive to achieve anything if it will all be wiped out?

Death profoundly influences man's perception of value and meaning. But it needn't always be negative. For, contrary to popular opinion, death is not an adversary. It is a friend and ally. It creates meaning because it sets limits. Experience becomes valuable because it is bounded with time.

If life has meaning then so, too, must there certainly be a meaning to death.

THE SEVENTH SEAL

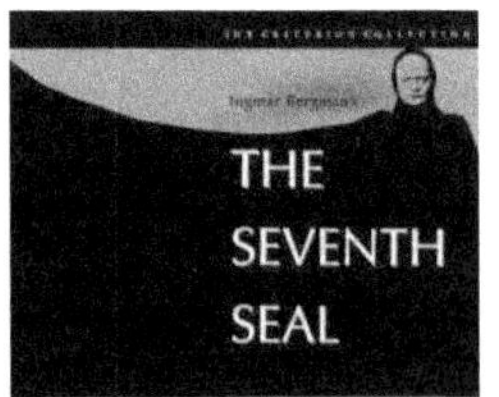

Director: Ingmar Bergman
Producer: Allan Ekelund
Screenplay: Ingmar Bergman
From the screenplay "Painting on Wood" based on the play Sculpture in Wood both by Ingmar Bergman
1957 B & W
Swedish with English subtitles

The Seventh Seal is Bergman's apocalyptic vision of man's passage through life and confrontation with death. It is the ultimate "meaning-of-life" movie. The symbolism and structure of the film are both simple and elegant.

Returning in dismay from his idealistic crusade, Antonius Block (Max von Sydow) and his squire are confronted by the Black Death which is ravaging Europe. The squire, Jöns (Gunnar Björnstrand), asks directions from a monk seated on the ground. With no answer, he grabs him and realizes it is a corpse. He remounts his horse, and his master asks if the monk showed him the way.

"He was most eloquent," answers Jöns wryly, "but very gloomy."

And so, from the beginning, lies the thinly-disguised premise of Bergman's film. The protagonist seeks guidance from a corpse, from Death—and he receives no response. The corpse was that of a monk—a representative of the religion that had sent both knight and squire off on their crusade. Does this mean that their religion is dead? The witty, and more down-to-earth squire remarks that the answer was most eloquent. Like a Zen parable replete with meaning, the nothingness bespeaks myriad allusions.

In a seeming shadow of Cervantes, the Crusader knight and his squire are like Don Quixote and Sancho Panza. Just as Don Quixote set off on his idealistic quest, so too did Antonius Block. Just as Sancho Panza is more earthly and practical, so too is Block's squire.

And Block, just like Don Quixote, seems to have come to his senses in the end. Returning from the Crusades, he is disillusioned over his "cause." He is despondent over all the suffering and killing. He is distressed by the Black

Death that is plaguing Christendom—almost as though all Europe is being punished for its sins.

Like Sancho Panza, the knight's squire realizes all their efforts were a sham. He catches the theological seminarist, Raval (now turned petty thief), as he steals from his hapless victims. This seminarist had persuaded Block and Jöns to go off on their ten-year, religious crusade. What hypocrisy, what lies and deceit—when he stays home; steals from the dead; bullies others; and attempts to rape a peasant girl.

From the opening scene of the movie Antonius Block is confronted by Death. The Grim Reaper has arrived to take the Crusader knight away. But Block is conniving. He seduces Death into playing a game of chess. As long as the game continues, Antonius may live. If he wins, his life will be spared. If he loses, then Death can take him away. Death cannot refuse. He loves to play games.

Throughout the film, the game is played intermittently on a metaphysical plane. While others go about the business of life, Death and the knight play quietly off to the side. Fate is being determined while the common man remains oblivious.

Antonius uses the brief respite of the game to unravel the meaning of his life. It seems all to have been "vanity and a striving after the wind." His squire now becomes his mentor, explaining the meaninglessness of existence amidst the knight's disillusionment.

The knight and squire continue their journey; meet other fellow travelers along the path of life; and take part in a number of diversions and escapades. A young, cheerful couple (itinerant actors with a baby) join the knight before entering a dark, dangerous forest. Of all the companions, they seem to represent the best promise for mankind.

As the film nears its finale, the troupe encounters the burning of a so-called witch—an innocent, deranged girl whom the Inquisition blames for bringing the plague. Antonius knows that she cannot escape her death, for no one can. The most he can do is offer a potion that will ease her pain.

As the knight and squire watch the girl burn, Jöns—the real mentor—instructs Antonius to look into her eyes. It is not the horror of Hell or the Devil she sees. It is the horror of the nothingness. Bergman's film portrays the existential response to the emptiness of life.

Meanwhile, the metaphysical chess game is also nearing its conclusion. Antonius is losing. He knows there is no way out. At the same time the young actor (who has been chided for "seeing visions") suddenly notices Antonius and Death playing chess off to the side. Death has hinted that perhaps all of the knight's companions will be forfeit if he loses. And so, without hope, Antonius abruptly turns and his swirling cape overturns the chess pieces.

"I'm sorry, I've forgotten their positions."

"But I have not," dryly remarks Death.

Death replaces the pieces and then checkmates the knight with the next move. In the meantime, the young couple and their baby take off in the wagon, fleeing from the apparition of Death.

"You lose," says Death. "It was all for nothing."

"Maybe not," answers Antonius. "It was a distraction."

The distraction provided time for the knight to come to terms with Death, as well as with the meaning of his life. The distraction had also allowed the young family to escape Death's clutches. The one optimistic, cheerful, and romantic face in the film will live on. Rather than a totally bleak and depressing vision, Bergman ends his movie with the promise of hope.

Although death is inevitable, a happy life of affirmation can trump Death after all. Although pain and suffering are rampant like the plague, its effects can be softened and comforted with compassion. Just as Antonius could not stop the young girl from being burned at the stake, he could at least ease her torment.

What Bergman seems to be saying is that in the chess game of life, Death always has the last play. The most that can be hoped for is a good and challenging game.

"Your move."

CHUSHINGURA

The Loyal 47 Samurai

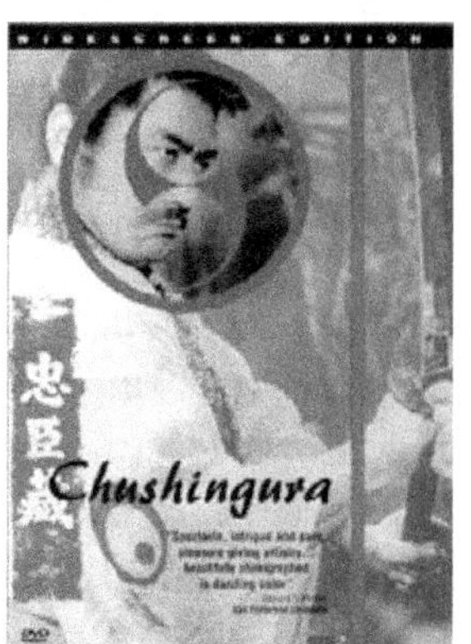

Director: Hiroshi Inagaki
Producer: Hiroshi Inagaki, Sanezumi Fujimoto & Yomoyuki Tanaka
Screenplay: Toshio Yasumi
1962 Color
Japanese with English subtitles

One must understand that Chushingura is a film from a different culture. And it is a foreign culture as it was three centuries in the past. Codes of honor and behavior are sadly lacking in modern-day, western culture. Whereas, loyalty and honor meant everything to the samurai. Respect and dignity meant everything to the ruling class.

Now, a brief history lesson. Peace has reigned for over a century in Japan. Previously, clans were in a continual state of warfare. However, once the most powerful shogun took control, he united Japan under one rule. The emperor became a figurehead.

To enforce the peace, many restrictions were placed upon time-honored samurai values. For example, it was now against the law for a samurai or his clan to take revenge. The shogunate meted out justice, and its judgment was final. Violating its decree was punishable by death. This ensured that the feuding families would think twice before avenging some petty slight. Not only would the violator be executed, but his family clan would be dishonored, and their estates would be confiscated. Thus, the shogunate grew richer and more powerful, while keeping Japan in relative peace.

Chushingura: the Loyal 47 Samurai is a powerful movie about an incident that took place in March 1701 Japan. The incident has become legendary. It has spawned numerous books, plays, songs, short stories, as well as over twenty films of which Chushingura is likened to Gone with the Wind as an epic classic.

The movie begins with two rival officials in feudal Japan: Lord Kira (Master of Ceremonies in the Shogun's palace) and Lord Asano (new Head of Reception). Kira is to teach the newly-appointed Asano his duties. He wants the customary gifts and bribes, but Asano believes bribery to be the root of government corruption. He therefore offers only a token gift which angers Kira.

While in the Shogun's palace, Kira insults and taunts Asano into drawing his sword and attacking. This is a capital offense: merely to draw a sword in the Shogun's palace (much less spill blood) is punishable by death. By official decree the offender must commit seppuku (ritual suicide). Asano does so out of obedience and honor. His clan is enraged and vow to avenge their master. Kira (who survived his injury) is on alert as well as the police and the Shogun's army. But to everyone's surprise the Asano castle is surrendered peacefully. The Asano clan dissipates, disbands since it no longer has a leader. Many become destitute, lead a life of debauchery and drunkenness. They seemingly no longer pose a threat. They no longer seem to care. But in reality . . .

In reality it is all a ruse to lure the Kira clan into a false sense of security. The 47 ronin (master-less samurai) have actually strengthened their vow of vengeance. But, knowing that reprisal is expected, they bide their time—waiting patiently for the enemy to drop their guard.

For more than a year and a half they meet secretly, planning their strategy of attack. They sign a pact in blood that their cause is to the death. For even those who survive the battle will likely be bound to commit seppuku. The police will be after them anyway. The Shogun's army, by official decree, will execute them for their willful defiance. So they know full well that death will have the final word.

The knowledge that they are all dead men anyway (whether or not they survive) makes them awesome warriors. Twenty-one months after their master's death they storm Lord Kira's castle, taking everyone by surprise. Like the wind they sweep through the compound killing anyone who takes up arms and resists. Though originally far outnumbered, they nevertheless subdue the enemy without a single fatality among themselves. Lord Kira is found hiding. He refuses to commit seppuku, and so he is promptly executed. His head is mounted atop a pole, and the 47 ronin march defiantly through town to their master's grave. Here, the movie ends. But the legend of the 47 ronin continues.

The police hear of the atrocity and blockade the bridge to the cemetery. But the ronin are dauntless. They have vowed to plant Kira's head at the foot of Lord Asano's grave, and nothing must stand in their way. The police realize they are dealing with an unearthly power. They know that nothing they do will stop these dead men from reaching their goal. The police respectfully move aside, allowing the ronin to pass.

The trophy is planted. The ronin are arrested and allowed to commit mass seppuku (the largest in Japanese history). But honor has been served. Their master's soul can rest in peace as well as 47 of their own. The legend is passed down through the hearts and minds of future generations and becomes part of Japanese culture and heritage. A national shrine is built where the 47 ronin are interred with their master. Pilgrimages are made and incense is kept burning to memorialize and honor these 47 heroes.

The moral is one of loyalty, stealth and patience, courage and will power—but also of the incredible strength and fearlessness that can be generated out of an acceptance of one's fate, an embracing of one's death. For it is our fear of death that weakens and fills us with trepidation. Accepting death, as do the samurai, empowers and strengthens.

In Chushingura, director Hiroshi Inagaki has created the best film version of the 47 ronin story. Although modern western culture, even modern-day Japan, may scowl at this glorification of killing and revenge, something deep within our psyche still is awed and respectful. Perhaps it is a lingering archetype from the past when codes of honor meant everything. Perhaps, in this contemporary world of shifting loyalties, part of our soul longs for a world where one follows loyalty even to death. Dying for a cause, for justice, for one's clan, for one's Lord. This samurai spirit has survived undaunted for centuries, even though the samurai, themselves, are a thing of the past.

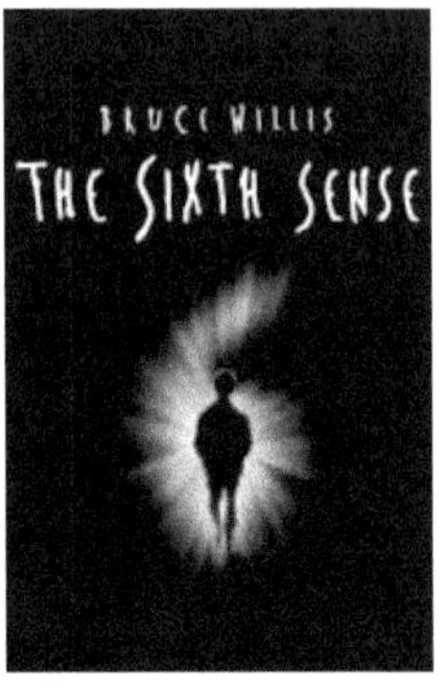

THE SIXTH SENSE

Director: M. Night Shyamalan
Producer: Frank Marshall, Kathleen Kennedy & Barry Mendel
Screenplay: M. Night Shyamalan
1999 Color

There is a saying among "Fourth Way" schools (Gurdjieff in particular) that if one knew for certain the day and year one would die—one's life would change instantly. One's priorities would shift drastically. One would begin to realize what is really important. People can't foresee their death. But they can pretend to see their death. They can also pretend to see their life.

When death approaches, how different things look. How treasured is each moment as life nears its end? How precious are loved ones who will be left behind? Have things been left undone? Things left unsaid? Would one live any differently? While not addressing these questions specifically, The Sixth Sense evokes a nostalgic wistfulness about a life that might have been.

Director/writer M. Night Shyamalan creates a movie about life and death. The soul survives bodily death, and haunts familiar abodes until spiritual resolution is achieved. Those sensitive enough can see this other-worldly presence overlaid on the normal, human world.

The movie begins on a night when child psychologist Malcolm Crowe (Bruce Willis) receives an award for service to his community. A distraught, former patient (now grown to a young man) breaks into the doctor's home. He accuses Malcolm of failing him and not keeping his promise. He then shoots Malcolm, and then himself, all in front of Malcolm's wife.

Within a year, Malcolm takes on the case of a troubled nine-year-old boy. Cole (Haley Joel Osment) has problems at school, with teachers and other children, and even with his mother. Malcolm draws the boy out from his shell, and eventually wins his trust.

"I want to tell you my secret now."

"Okay."

"I see dead people."

"In your dreams?" Cole shakes his head.
"While you're awake?" Cole nods. "Dead people like in graves,
in coffins?" asks Malcolm.

"Walking around like regular people.
They don't see each other. They only see what they want to see.
They don't know they're dead."

"How often do you see them?"

"All the time. They're everywhere."

Malcolm realizes Cole is seriously disturbed. He may need medication and hospitalization. But eventually Malcolm has second thoughts, and finally is convinced of Cole's abilities. Malcolm becomes a believer. Cole really does have a special gift. Malcolm helps Cole to face his fears and confront the ghosts. "They just want help. . . . Listen to them."

Despite initial horrifying events, Cole listens and learns and helps the dead find resolution. They can pass on peacefully to another realm. Cole becomes happier and more outgoing. He isn't as frightened since he knows the dead just need his help.

Cole and Malcolm meet for one last session. They both realize the therapy has been a success. They won't see each other again, although Cole says, "Maybe we can pretend . . ." Cole goes on to reveal his secret to his mother. In an emotionally convincing display she becomes a believer.

The unexpected twist comes at the end of the movie. While standing over the sleeping, dreaming body of his wife, a ring drops from her hand and rolls toward Malcolm. It is his wedding band. He looks at his own hand. It's not there. He never takes it off!

A look of incredulity and shock flashes over his face. His mind is assimilating and evaluating what he thought was his life. He realizes in one dreadful moment that he is dead. He never recovered from the gunshot wound last year. For the past year he has been a ghost haunting the living world of his wife. No wonder she can't forget, can't move on with her life. The melancholy awareness allows him to let go and say good-bye.

Malcolm needed Cole in order to realize that he himself was really dead. And Cole needed Malcolm to realize that the dead weren't necessarily mean and scary, that they might just need his help. And so the movie ends with Malcolm fading into a white light with the image of his wife on their wedding day.

The Sixth Sense is a spiritual thriller about death and the afterlife. Director M. Night Shyamalan has succeeded in creating an unpredictable twist that changes the whole tone of the movie. From a conventional ghost story plot one is suddenly transported to a metaphysical, unearthly viewpoint. Oh, my God! He's really dead! He's a ghost who just thinks he's alive!

How many of us just think we're alive?

IKIRU

(To Live)

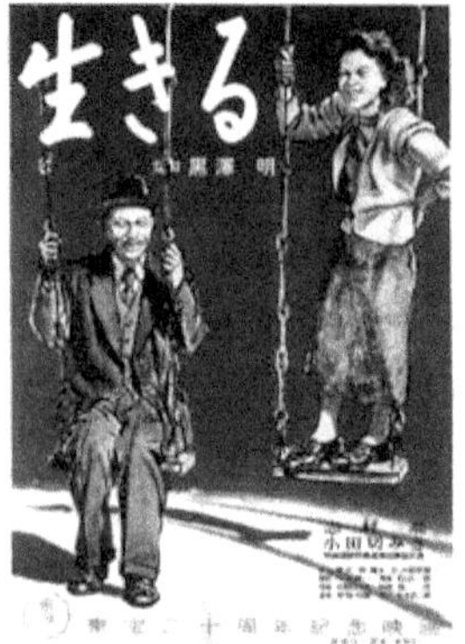

Director: Akira Kurosawa
Producer: Shojiro Motoki
Screenplay: Akira Kurosawa, Shinobu Hashimoto & Hideo Oguni
1952 B & W
Japanese with Enlgish subtitles

What is the meaning of life? How much time do we waste in meaningless triviality? If we knew death was imminent, how would it affect our lives? As the Russian mystic-philosopher Gurdjieff maintained: our lives would change instantly. Director Akira Kurosawa shows, in Ikiru, just how radically life can alter when death looms literally by one's side.

Kanji Watanabe (Takashi Shimura) is the chief of the Citizens Section at the local Municipal Office. He has worked there for almost thirty years. Monotonous, boring, and meaningless paper-shuffling. He is in a lifelong rut which would normally end in an empty, mundane retirement. However, something is troubling Kanji. His stomach begins to hurt.

An examination by doctors tells him he has a slight ulcer. But another patient tells him the medical staff always lie. He describes the symptoms in the development of stomach cancer, and Kanji realizes he has not long to live. No longer than six months at most.

Kanji's life changes drastically. He fails to appear at work. Doesn't even give notice. Previously he had not missed a day of work in thirty years. Day after day he is absent. Finally he reports that he is ill and takes a leave of absence.

Kanji reevaluates his life and realizes he hasn't really lived. He had been a mindless automaton doing his duty for thirty years. Since he is dying anyway, he withdraws 50,000 yen from his life savings and decides to live it up. But he doesn't know how.

Luckily, he meets a young writer who is fascinated by his predicament. He offers to be Kanji's Mephistopheles, and show him how to enjoy life. The writer shows Kanji around the town: bars, nightclubs, dance halls, stage-shows, gambling casinos, burlesque, and loose women. Kanji is happy for awhile, but eventually seems to just be going through the motions in a drunken stupor.

Finally Kanji is rescued by Toyo Odagiri, a woman co-worker who wants to resign, but needs his seal to make it official. They go to his home where everyone believes he has taken on a young mistress. That's where all the time and money are going! Toyo makes it believable since she is so bubbly and overflowing with life. Kanji is drawn to her vitality and optimism. In fact, the reason she wants to quit is that she sees her job as a life-draining dead end.

Kanji and Toyo go to movies and restaurants, skating rinks and nightclubs. They have fun for awhile, but eventually the magic wears off. She becomes bored. She finds it unnatural. On their last date he tells her about his condition. He doesn't know what life is all about. He never really lived.

Toyo explains, that's why she quit her job and took up a new one. Now she makes furry, toy, bunny rabbits that hop around for little children. She feels she's made friends with all the babies in Japan. "Why don't you do something like that, too?" she asks. "It's too late," he says despondently. But then slowly, a wild crazy look burns in his eyes. "It isn't too late! . . . if I'm really determined."

Kanji returns to his office and works on a citizens' proposal to drain an area of land and build a local children's park. The half-dozen women behind the proposal have been getting nothing but the bureaucratic runaround. When Kanji takes up the proposal, he too gets the runaround. But he is a section chief, has some influence, and with persistence he finally pushes the proposal through. The park is built. Generations of children will now have somewhere to play and have fun. Kanji's life has garnered some vestige of meaning.

Kanji dies soon after the park is built. It is as though he were just hanging on to see its completion. "It seemed as if only his work kept Watanabe alive." A policeman at the wake tells how he saw Kanji swinging in the park on his last night on earth. "But, he looked so happy." It is the most tear-jerking scene in the movie. Kanji swings slowly, singing the melancholy song, "Life is Brief."* But in the end, he accomplished all that he set out to do. He is found the next day, dead of gastric cancer, in the beautiful little park that he built.

The women who proposed the park appear at the wake, sobbing mournfully. They seem more upset than his own son or daughter-in-law, or any of his co-workers. Perhaps, because only they could appreciate what his life had meant—how he had suffered and died trying to accomplish something that would make others happy.

Akira Kurosawa masterfully portrays how the knowledge of impending death can affect one's life. Kanji's life and death serve as an inspiration to his co-workers. "Let's work hard!" "Yes, with the same spirit as Watanabe!" "We mustn't let his death be in vain." Kanji, himself, had virtually no life to speak of, until his last six months when he learned what it really means "To Live."

* This is Kanji's name for the song, "Gondola no Uta" ("Song of the Gondola"), composed by Shimpei Nakayama in 1915 with lyrics by Izamu Yoshi.

CHAPTER ELEVEN

PARADISE & TRANSCENDENCE

The ultimate goal of human consciousness is known by various names: Nirvana, Samadhi, Paradise, Shangri-La. It is the final stage of bliss where the soul, at last, finds its home—where it finds solace surrounded by an atmosphere of oneness and peace. All is forgiven, understood, and accepted. The meaning of life is to be—transcended.

XANADU

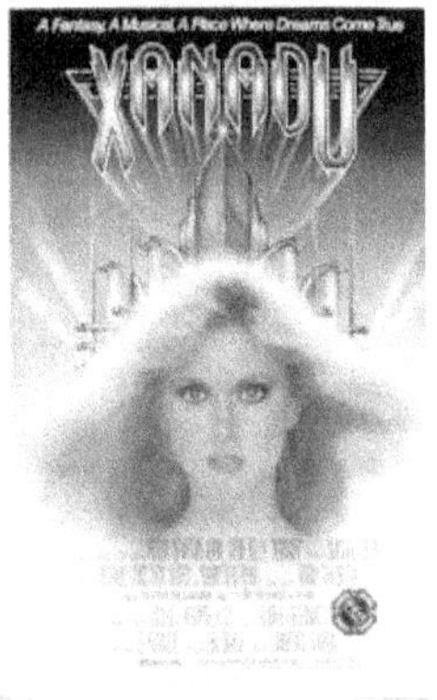

Director: Robert Greenwald
Producer: Lawrence Gordon
Written by Richard Danus & Marc Rubel
1980 Color

"In Xanadu did Kubla Khan
A stately pleasure-dome decree:
Where Alph, the sacred river, ran
Through caverns measureless to man
Down to a sunless sea."

Samuel Taylor Coleridge, the author of "Kubla Khan," may have remembered only half of his famous poem. But Danus and Rubel, in the movie Xanadu, surely provided the other half that was forgotten. While the film can be viewed as "quaint" or "dated" or even "corny," the theme of inspired idealism pervades the story with the simple adage: remember and live your dreams.

Sonny (Michaeal Beck) is a young, aspiring artist who is dismayed by having to prostitute his talents to commercial art. While wandering through a seaside park he meets a retired big-band musician, Danny (Gene Kelly), who tells him of his dream of opening a night club. The plan excites Sonny, for he needs a change from his spiritually-deadening job. He decides to quit and join together their resources to make Danny's dream of Xanadu come true—an entertainment palace fit for the gods.

In the meantime, Sonny keeps running into a mysterious, young woman, Kira (Olivia Newton-John). Synchronicity and mutual attraction seem to be pulling them together. But Kira is not what she appears.

On the brick wall of a dead-end street is a giant, Greek mural depicting the nine muses of the arts—something Sonny himself could have or should have painted. Unbeknownst to Sonny, Kira is herself one of the nine muses. She had emerged from the mural, coming to life to guide both Sonny and Danny. Hence her appearance on earth coincides with Sonny's decision to quit, as well as Danny's commitment to create his dream. For the Greek muses were daughters of Zeus, sent to inspire mankind through the creative arts.

When a writer has his "block;" when a musician cannot compose; when an artist stares depressingly at his empty canvas, it is because his muse has left him. He has no inspiration. With Sonny's commitment to Xanadu, his muse has returned. The energy, the sense of excitement, the overflowing enthusiasm is akin to love. Sonny finds himself falling in love with Kira. And she, too, falls in love with the mere mortal she was sent simply to inspire. And thus, the stage is set for the ministrations of the Fates (also goddesses in Greek mythology).

With hard work, Xanadu becomes a reality. Everyone joins in to make it manifest on the physical plane—a feat on par with the gods—creating something out of nothing. For, after all, Xanadu was originally just a poet's dream.

But now that the work of art is complete, Kira must return to Mount Helicon. For she lives and belongs in the ethereal realm of the gods—not in the mundane world of everyday human reality. Oh yes, she can visit now and then to inspire mortals to create and dream. But she herself cannot exist permanently on earth, or so the gods say.

"Dreams die," says Sonny despondently after Kira has left.

"No. No. No," says Danny. "Not by themselves. . . . We kill them." He urges Sonny to keep the faith, to pursue his dream.

Sonny thus enters through the Greek mural and reaches Mount Helicon. He finds Kira and pleads with her and Zeus, but to no avail. Zeus forbids it! Kira cannot remain on earth. Her task is complete. The two young lovers must be parted—forever? Or for a day? Zeus forgets.

The opening night for Xanadu is a huge success. The dream has become manifest, made palpable and real. Sonny, though, is in a blue funk. Although trying to put on a brave face, he has been devastated by the Fates. But are the Fates so cruel? For those who follow their dreams is this the reward or punishment—to love and long for, only to be parted—to have a taste of true happiness only to have it brusquely withdrawn?

Director Robert Greenwald's finale is a finale of the creative spirit. Dance routines and musical numbers flash past with Kira starring in every possible role. From pretty cowgirl in boots and cowboy hat, to a twenties flapper, to a wild and sexy cat woman. Her persona is varied, her roles transform her dress and mystique. It is a phantasmagoria—a kaleidoscope of all possible performances changing with a sleight of hand.

Sonny is happy that everyone else is happy, but he himself is still sad.

Greenwald directs the final shot in a masterful denouement. A cocktail waitress arrives at Sonny's table with a drink. Sonny does a double-take. Is it Kira? If it is, she's not letting on. She's smiling, knowingly(?), as Sonny engages her in conversation.

Did Kira defy Zeus and return to earth? Has she become mortal and lost her contact with the divine? Sonny isn't sure. But does it really even matter? Kira, a muse, in her many guises can manifest in any number of forms. Which is the true Kira? Sonny smiles at the trickster element of Kira. He'll play along because he now realizes that Kira, his dream, his inspiration, his muse, shines like a many-faceted diamond on the material plane. The sparkle of the ideal flashes and glitters with each new perspective.

"In Xanadu did Kubla Khan
A stately pleasure-dome decree:
Where Alph, the sacred river, ran
Through caverns measureless to man
Down to a sunless sea."

Unknown to most theater-goers, Samuel Taylor Coleridge claimed that his poem, "Kubla Khan," came to him in a dream—not inspired or loosely based upon, but directly narrated and transcribed from a dream.

In the midst of frantically recalling and recording the poem, Coleridge was interrupted by a visitor to his home. After the guest had left, Coleridge sat back down at his writing table, but the flow of words had ceased. The dream had vanished.

Although "Kubla Khan" is a classic, widely acclaimed and famous for its dream origin, Coleridge estimated that half the poem was lost. "Kubla Khan" itself, along with the mythical realm of Xanadu, originated in the ideal dream-world of artistic inspiration. The poem was Kira's message from the divine. And the ideal message was translated and transformed into the fantasia of "Xanadu." And Xanadu then manifested as a hit-song and a movie.

When time passes, when youth fades, when idealism gives way to practicality, when inspiration is jaded by the school of hardknocks—Xanadu is a refreshing, encouraging, and inspiriting call from beyond. Never give up your idealism. Follow your dreams and make them real. For glimmers of the ideal pervade the world. Kira's sparkling message of hope and optimism can be seen in any number of persons, places, or things.

In a fitting tribute to the artistic muses that helped make his career in film, in song, and in dance, Xanadu was the last dance performance on screen of Gene Kelly's illustrious life. The cycle is complete and comes to a closing circle in Xanadu: the creative, artistic dream-world of the gods.

"Building your dream
Has to start now.
There's no other road to take.
You won't make a mistake.
I'll be guiding you."

LOST HORIZON

Director: Frank Capra
Producer: Frank Capra
Screenplay: Robert Riskin from the novel Lost Horizon by James Hilton
1937 B & W

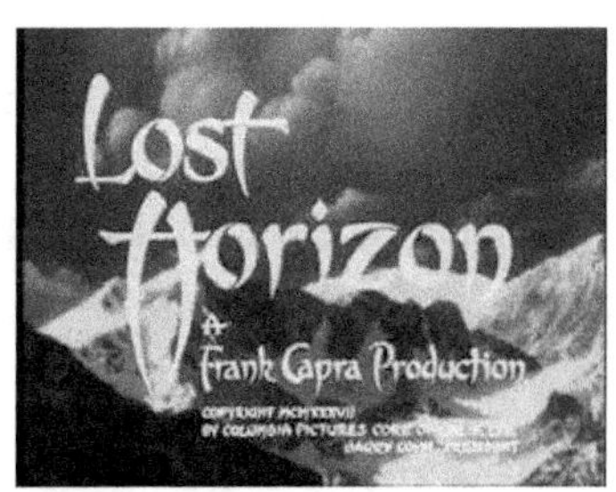

All men, in all places, throughout time, have dreamt or fantasized about the ideal world—a paradise where man lives in harmony with nature, where peace and brotherhood and mutual respect govern the land. It is an archetype in man's psyche: the longing for utopia. In the classic movie and novel, Lost Horizon, director Frank Capra and writer James Hilton bring this paradise-on-earth to life.

The movie begins with an evacuation of white foreigners during a revolutionary uprising in China. Soldier-hero/diplomat Robert Conway (Ronald Colman) and four evacuees are hijacked and taken deep into Tibet. They crash-land and are rescued by villagers from a remote, hidden monastery. The survivors are provided shelter and hospitality in the unbelievable paradise of Shangri-La.

The utopian community is nestled in the beautiful "Valley of the Blue Moon," protected on all sides by towering mountain ranges. It is the Garden of Eden: mild climate, bountiful harvests.

From the moment of arrival, Conway finds himself attracted to Sondra (Jane Wyatt), another rescued adventurer who has grown to cherish the ideals and principles of Shangri-La. They begin falling in love with each other. Conway is at peace. He wants to remain in Shangri-La. In his own words from his own book: "There are moments in every man's life when he glimpses the eternal."

However, it turns out that the hijacking and "rescue" were all orchestrated by Shangri-La. Conway confides to Sondra that, although he has been kidnapped, he feels amiable about the situation. He wonders why.

"Perhaps because you've always been a part of Shangri-La without knowing it."

"I wonder," says Conway.

"I'm sure of it, just as I'm sure there's a wish for Shangri-La in everyone's heart."

But the others don't feel so cozy in paradise, especially when they discover they had been kidnapped. Conway's own brother, George, is the most adamant about leaving. He agitates and tries to get the others to side with his plan to escape. He doesn't want to go alone. For it is a dangerous trek through the snowy, mountain pass.

Meanwhile, Conway has an interview with the High Lama. It is revealed that he is the original founder of Shangri-La. He is a Belgian priest, a Father Perrault who is over two hundred years old. One of the fringe benefits of peaceful coexistence in paradise is an extremely long life span.

Father Perrault tries to persuade Conway to join him in governing Shangri-La. For he reveals that he has not long to live. Someone like Conway is needed to carry on his vision. And what was his mission? To create a safe harbor for the best mankind had to offer. For over two centuries Father Perrault had collected music, literature, and art. When the world has finished destroying itself, Shangri-La can emerge like a shining beacon—the sole repository of hope for a better way of life. "I am placing in your hands the future and destiny of Shangri-La. For I am going to die."

Father Perrault dies in an ecstatic vision and is at peace. But Conway is now torn. He himself wants to stay, but his brother is dead-set upon leaving Shangri-La. He will be alone because the three other fellow-travelers wish to remain.

Conway has further doubts when another stranded foreigner, Maria (who loves George), tells her story. Shangri-La is no paradise. They brought her here against her will. She's a prisoner, just like George. She hates it here. She'd give anything to leave. Her testimony is successful. Conway agrees to go with them. For it was wrong to kidnap people against their will.

The three leave Shangri-La and join up with hired porters on the plateau above the Valley of the Blue Moon. They struggle through the frozen terrain, through blizzards and across snowfields, all the while falling farther behind the porters. Eventually the porters are swept away in an avalanche.

The climax to the movie comes when Maria turns into an old hag. They were all warned she would become old if she left the beneficent influence of Shangri-La. But Maria claimed it was a lie, for she was a recent arrival to the monastery. Now, both Conway and George realize the claims of Shangri-La were true. George becomes hysterical and flings himself off a cliff. Conway is left to find his way out of the Himalayas—the sole survivor of the expedition.

Conway is rescued, but while being brought back to civilization he escapes. He makes his way back to the Himalayas, trying again and again to penetrate through the raging blizzards and snowslides. Eventually, after a half dozen attempts, he disappears into the mountains, never again to be seen.

Back in civilization, the man who had been tracking Conway is questioned by his peers:

> "What do you think of his talk about Shangri-La? Do you believe it?"
>
> "Yes. Yes, I believe it. I believe it because I want to believe it.
> Gentlemen, I give you a toast.
> Here's my hope that Robert Conway will find his Shangri-La.
> Here's my hope that we all find our Shangri-La."

And the movie ends, showing us Conway, standing in triumph at the hidden pass overlooking Shangri-La. He had found his way home. After a period of doubt, he regained his vision of a utopian dream.

Frank Capra and James Hilton bring to the screen an image buried within all men's souls—a hope and longing for a world of peace, love, and camaraderie. It is the promise of all religions—a paradise exempt from all earthly strife. Capra and Hilton tapped into a universal archetype, which is why Lost Horizon will remain a favorite for all time.

MEETINGS WITH REMARKABLE MEN

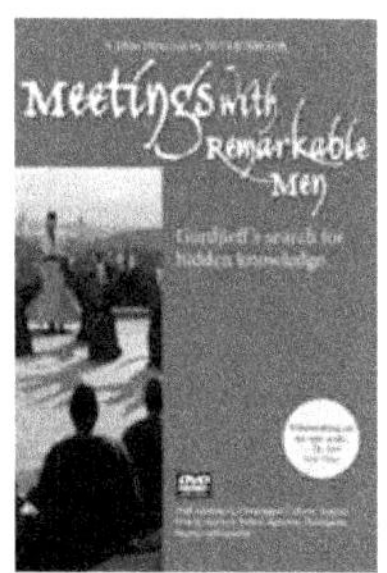

Director: Peter Brook
Producer: Stuart Lyons
Screenplay: Jeanne de Salzmann & Peter Brook
From the book by George Ivanovitch Gurdjieff
1979 Color

"I want to know why I am here," proclaims the protagonist of the film, George Ivanovitch Gurdjieff (Dragan Maksimovic). The movie is based on the early memoirs of his search for truth. Gurdjieff was the founder of a school of thought known as the "Fourth Way." Some consider his following a cult, others a philosophy of life. In any case, Gurdjieff and Ouspensky and other Fourth Way schools exist to this day. The film, created by some of his followers, explores Gurdjieff's quest through the Middle East and central Asia.

Mysterious and enigmatic. Gurdjieff came to Paris and London teaching a system of thought and physical movements that he learned in the East. The arcane knowledge was taught by an esoteric order known as the Sarmoun Brotherhood hidden somewhere in the mountains of central Asia. The Sarmoun was ancient, founded in Babylon 2,500 years before Christ.

The movie begins with Gurdjieff as a boy (Mikica Dimitrijevic). He witnesses unusual events that have mysterious explanations. In one scene, a musical competition is held once every twenty years in a unique canyon. Only a divine musician can make the canyon walls reverberate with the voice of God. Both musical instruments and human song are employed by various contestants to win the title. Failure after failure. But eventually one contestant's voice resonates with the harmonics of the canyon. Echo after echo rings out and fades away.

In another instance, a Yezidi boy is entrapped inside a chalk circle. He cannot get out no matter how much he, or others, try. Finally, young Gurdjieff breaks the circle by erasing part of the line with his shoe. The boy then runs off, escaping his captors and tormentors.

In yet another instance, a dead man rises overnight and is found lying at the village well. His spirit wouldn't rest. The village elder kills him for a second time with a knife.

Now, a young man, Gurdjieff combines forces with other seekers of truth. "Nothing will stop us until we find an answer." They pull scams to raise money in order to buy volumes of old books. But the truth isn't there. Yet a clue is mentioned, as well as on an old scroll found in a clay pot: the Sarmoun Brotherhood.

Gurdjieff travels to Egypt where he meets a Russian prince who is also on the same quest. Gurdjieff is encouraged and excited at the possibility of attaining his goal. "Ever since I was a child, I had the feeling that something is missing in me. I felt that apart from my ordinary life there is another life—a life that is calling me."

The prince leaves with a dervish, and Gurdjieff is again alone. He joins up with a professor, an archaeologist seeking the wisdom of an ancient library buried somewhere in the Gobi desert. They gather guides and other friends to form an expedition. But eventually, after much hardship and disaster, all the fellow travelers disband and go their own way.

Finally, Gurdjieff and the professor connect with someone willing to introduce them to the Sarmoun Brotherhood. The professor stays behind with the dervish. But Gurdjieff is taken blindfolded through miles of desert and canyons. Eventually, after days of travel, they arrive at the tranquil, monastic school.

The followers of the Sarmoun engage in unusual physical movements and dances. Some dances look like the precursor for those of the famous whirling dervishes. Others are jerky, awkward pantomimes designed to train the mind and coordinate the body. Each body posture is a symbol from an ancient language which everyone in the monastery understands.

The method of body-mind philosophy is akin to yoga and tai-chi. The movements thus have a credible basis in practices rooted a thousand years in the past. To discipline the body and mind together, only then will the spirit gain true freedom.

The body discipline first teaches one to know what one is, where one is, how one is doing what one does. The mental discipline eliminates extraneous distractions, teaching one who one is, and why one exists. The spiritual discipline teaches one to be aware of the present moment. It generates power of life and will. Needless to say, Gurdjieff remains for years to study and understand his being.

Meetings With Remarkable Men is a brief introduction to the Fourth Way schools of Gurdjieff, Ouspensky, Salzmann, Bennett and others. Gurdjieff was himself a remarkable man. Inevitable ego-clashes caused the final splintering of his group after his demise. But all who knew him considered Gurdjieff a charismatic and spiritually profound leader.

If there is a purpose to life, if man is here to evolve spiritually to a higher plane, then perhaps Gurdjieff and his Fourth Way point in generally the right direction. In any case, as the old adage goes: even a wrong direction is more enlightening than just drifting through life.

"Become yourself, then God and the Devil don't matter."

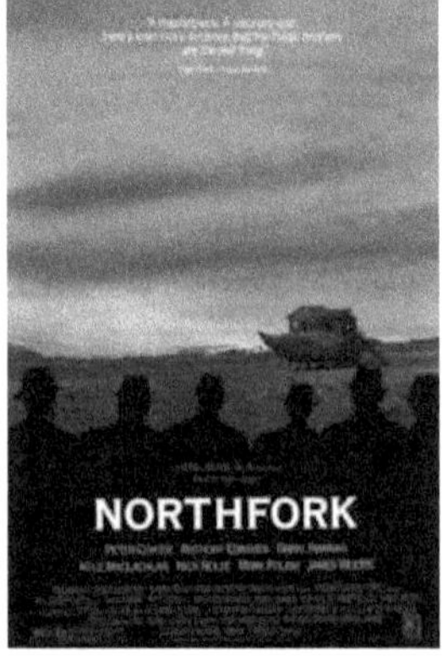

NORTHFORK

Director: Michael Polish
Producers: Mark Polish & Michael Polish
Screenplay: Mark Polish & Michael Polish
2003 Color

Northfork is a droll and whimsical film about the difficulty in giving up the earthly realm. Whether through death, or through mystical transcendence, man is hesitant to release his bonds to this world—perhaps because it is all we have ever known.

The movie is ostensibly about the effort to evacuate the town of Northfork. A dam and reservoir have been built which will eventually flood the entire valley.

The main plot is simply one of convincing the "hold-outs" to leave. While most residents have already relocated, a handful still remain. "Men-in-black" comprise several evacuation teams sent in for the final roundup.

Symbolism begins visually from the very start of the movie. Perhaps a prelude of the future, or perhaps a depiction of what is currently happening on another metaphysical plane, a black wooden coffin suddenly pops up out from the surface of a tranquil lake. It is the emergence of Death. The dead have arisen out of the waters of life. The coffin floats peacefully upon the surface like a lotus blossom—a blossom which represents the transcendent soul in eastern religions.

The movie itself is a metaphor for transcendence. In the beginning, is the emergence of death with the coffin. In the end, five of the more "enlightened" characters depart from earth by flying off in an airplane.

Angels are another symbol of the transcendental nature of the movie. They are the intermediary between the earthly realm and the heavenly. While at first it seems unlikely, the "men-in-black" evacuation teams are actually angels. They are aiding the suffering spirits of mortals to pass on to a higher level. In evicting people from their homes, they are actually helping them to transcend. For, while everyone desires the paradisiacal promise of heaven, how many would willingly go there—right now? Most of us are too comfortable and complacent in the mundane. Transcendence is frightening—because it is unknown.

Father Harlan (Nick Nolte) tries to inspire the residents of Northfork in his sermon: "But we will gain the hope, the courage, to move to a higher ground."

The leader of the evacuation teams also confirms this transcendental perspective:

> "Despite the tertiary inconveniences we're putting these people through, we're giving them new power."
>
> "You just come in like you're their guardian angel. You give them wings. And then you move them on up to higher ground."

The transcendental imagery is even apparent in the beginning of the movie.

The church is shown resting on a moving platform. Service is being held in a church without earthly foundation, since it, too, is preparing to transcend.

The subplot of the movie is the search for the "unknown angel." In what some may interpret as the delirium of a sick, dying boy—another realm or plane of existence is shown with the appearance of four colorful characters: an English aristocrat, "Cup of Tea;" a nerdy scholar and scientist, "Happy;" a strong, yet compassionate and hopeful athletic woman, "Flower Hercules;" and a quiet, American-looking cowboy complete with cowboy hat and boots, "Cod"—the strong, silent type who literally never says a word.

Almost all their appearances occur during the course of a little boy's (Irwin) illness. Could Irwin be the unknown angel? Flower Hercules believes and hopes it to be true. The others, however, remain skeptical until the end.

Father Harlan, while not partaking of these visions, nevertheless has no doubt that little Irwin is an angel. He says to Irwin's adoptive parents, "I gave you an angel." But he also believes, "We are all angels. It is what we do with our wings that separates us."

The thematic reality of the metaphysical realm of Cup of Tea, Happy, Flower Hercules, and Cod becomes apparent only at the very end of the movie. Walter (James Wood) and Willis, father and son, an evacuation team that the movie follows, are at the home of the last unconfirmed, hold-out residents in Northfork. The house is deserted, but both are uneasy because there is the "smell of death."

The film vacillates between shots of Walter and Willis searching the house, and the Heavenly quartet who are wary of the invaders. Walter is carrying a pair of supposed "angel" wings that the evacuation teams use as bribes or gifts for those they wish to depart. As he is urged by his son to jump across a five-foot gap in the de-constructed house, Walter stumbles and falls. The sudden impact awakens him to the world of the Heavenly quartet. They are concerned he may be injured (or momentarily dead)? But in the next moment he is back with his son Willis.

Spooked by the unearthly transition (although he is really an angel—perhaps he is intimidated by such close proximity to his superiors) Walter flees from the metaphysical residence and urges Willis to follow.

"Mark them down as departed," he nervously instructs Willis once they are back in their car. They leave the last house, but they also leave the angel wings that the Heavenly quartet require as proof. Irwin is an angel. And he is allowed to leave the earthly realm by dying and symbolically flying away to Heaven in an airplane.

Northfork is a unique film, both droll and fanciful, and yet spiritual and profound. The Polish brothers have created a simple vision with a simple message: you must let go and die, in a sense, in order to be reborn to a new life. You must release your grasp, forgo the security of this earthly realm, in order to transcend to the realm of the angels.

JACOB'S LADDER

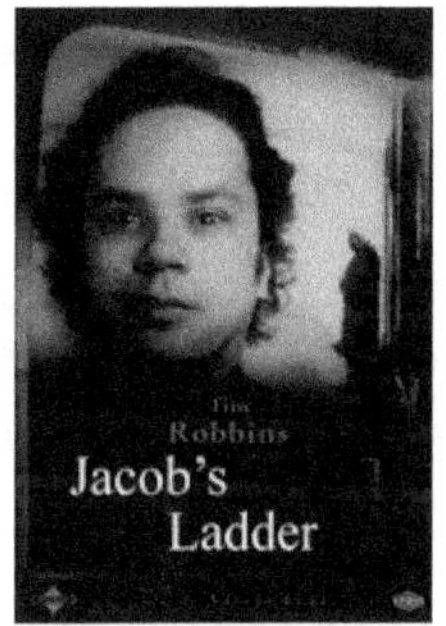

Director: Adrian Lyne
Producer: Alan Marshall
Screenplay: Bruce Joel Rubin
1990 Color

Just another paranoid-schizophrenic movie replete with demons and Vietnam flashbacks? Or perhaps something more? Director Adrian Lyne and writer Bruce Joel Rubin create something more—an hallucinogenic world of multiple realities and multiple personalities. Which is real? Is any of it real? Jacob Singer (Tim Robbins) must find out. Even if it means his life.

The movie begins in a conventional fashion: a Vietnam vet is having flashbacks of combat. He is now a New York postman riding home at night in the subway. He sees a demon: a drunk with a tail curling up under his clothes. A subway car filled with demons almost runs him over on the track. Dementia praecox begins.

Jake's new girlfriend, Jezzie, wants him to forget his past. She burns pictures of his ex-wife, Sarah, and their former married life. She wants him to let go, move on, try and forget—forget even Gabe, Jake's little boy, who had died in a car accident.

Something is happening. Jake becomes feverish, has hallucinations or visions of demons at a party, collapses screaming. Is he dying? The palm-reader at the party thinks so: "See, according to this, you're already dead. You're out of here, baby." But Jake continues to live. Jezzie saves him by dunking him in icy water to bring down his fever.

Meanwhile, Jake has been having flashbacks of Vietnam, of demons, and now of living with his ex-wife. Only she isn't an ex-wife, for they never got divorced. Jake tells Sarah that he dreamt he was living with Jezzie, his co-worker at the post office.

It all seems real and plausible, but the next moment he's back with Jezzie. What's happening? Is he hallucinating? Is he deranged? Which reality is real?

The demon-visions continue. They even try to run him down in a car. But now another element enters this paranoid world-view. A fellow Vietnam vet contacts Jake and tells him he, too, is being watched and followed. "I'm going to hell!" he claims in torment. For they are demons, and it's the only possible explanation. The next moment he is blown up with a car bomb. Jake's veteran doctor also died mysteriously when his car exploded. And now what? Is the government after his former battalion members? Do they want them all dead? Is it a conspiracy?

Jake and several other vets file a lawsuit against the government. They did something to them, perhaps a secret experiment. They all have the same symptoms. But in the next instant, they all turn against Jake. They drop the lawsuit. Their lawyer claims they never even went into battle. Everyone is against him. Jake is beaten "near death" and dumped on the street. Even Jezzie seems to turn on him because he is suspicious of her (after all, her name is Jezebel) despite all she's done to help.

Jake's one friend he can trust is Louis, his chiropractor. Through thick and thin he's always been there for him, straightening out his bones, giving him sage advice. "You know, you look like an angel, Louis? Like an overgrown cherub. . . . You're a lifesaver, Louis."

Louis even rescues Jake from the hospital of hellish horrors. He then counsels Jake about his brush with "near-death."

> "Am I dying, Louis? . . . I was in Hell. I don't want to die, Louis. . . . It's all pain."

> "You ever read Meister Eckhart?" asks Louis. "Eckhart saw Hell, too. You know what he said? He said, the only thing that burns in Hell is the part of you that won't let go of your life—your memories, your attachments.
>
> "They burn them all away. But they're not punishing you, he said. They're freeing your soul. . . .
>
> So the way he sees it: if you're frightened of dying and you're holding on, you'll see devils tearing your life away. But, if you've made your peace, then the devils are really angels freeing you from the earth.
>
> It's just a matter of how you look at it, that's all. So don't worry. Okay?"

The movie takes one more sudden turn. If multiple realities aren't confusing enough, another explanation is added for the viewer's total befuddlement. A chemist contacts Jake and tells him that he and his battalion were subject to a secret government experiment. During the last years of the war, the army felt that some drug was necessary to increase the fighting efficiency of the troops. They were too soft, lacked motivation. Something was needed to make them more aggressive, to tap their killer instinct.

A drug was developed and administered, and it worked, all too well. They murdered like maniacs gone berserk, killing everything, even themselves. The battalion virtually wiped themselves out. There was no enemy even present. It was all drug-induced fear, aggression, and hallucination.

The movie now turns from politics to metaphysics. Jacob returns to his old home and is greeted by the friendly doorman. He walks into the dimly-lit apartment and sits peacefully in thoughtful reverie on the couch. Suddenly he hears the music-box song "Sonny Boy" that was a favorite of his dead son Gabe. He rises and walks into the foyer to see Gabe playing at the bottom of the staircase. Jake is in ecstatic disbelief as he embraces his long-lost son. "It's okay. Come on, let's go up," says Gabe as he consolingly pats his dad on the back. They walk up the glowing stairway toward the light at the top of the landing.

The light becomes an overhead medical lamp. "He's gone," says the doctor. "He looks kind of peaceful . . . Put up a hell of a fight, though."

Jake was now dead from battle wounds in Vietnam. The entire movie was the hallucinatory flashback of a dying brain, a dying man, a dying soul. His memories and attachments were being burned away so that his soul could be freed, so that he could transcend.

> . . . Jacob slept at a place called Bethel, where he dreamed of a wonderful ladder between heaven and earth. In the dream, God promised to protect and bless Jacob and one day bring him home (Genesis 28: ll-17).[1]

Jacob's Ladder is a vision of what might happen during the moments before death. Director Adrian Lyne and writer Bruce Joel Rubin create a spine-tingling and metaphysically chilling preview of the near-death, after-life experience. Their philosophy and conclusion, as well as that of Meister Eckhart: In order to achieve peace and transcendence, one must no longer cling to life. One must release one's hold on all earthly attachment to find bliss. Is it true? Who can say? For those who die, mums the word.

---

1. The World Book Encyclopedia 2005 (Chicago: World Book, Inc., 2005), Volume ll, p. 19.

A VERY OLD MAN WITH ENORMOUS WINGS

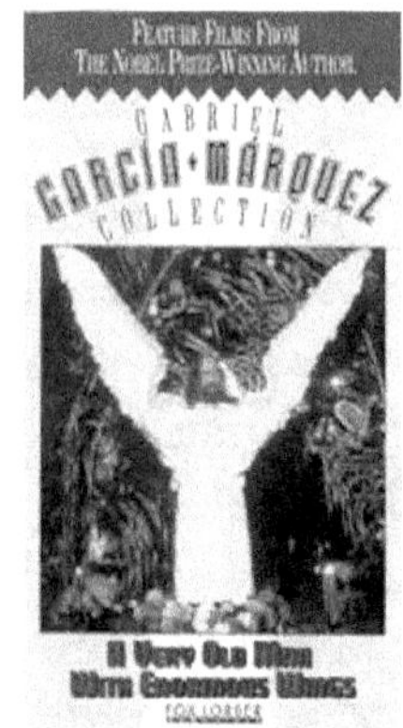

Director: Fernando Birri
Producer: Camilo Vives, Settimio Presutto & Luis Reneses
Screenplay: Gabriel Garcia Marquez & Fernando Birri
From the short story by Gabriel Garcia Marquez
1988 Color
Spanish with English subtitles

How many of us truly believe in miracles? Has modern man become so jaded that the miraculous no longer exists? Has science and technology corrupted our belief in the spiritual? Have we become too skeptical, lost our faith in the divine? If an angel came to earth would he be recognized or scoffed at? And Jesus Christ? Would the prophesied "second coming" be greeted with disdain?

In A Very Old Man with Enormous Wings, director Fernando Birri and Nobel Prize-winning author, Gabriel Garcia Marquez, paint a caricature of such an event. Even in a deeply religious, poor, rural village in South America, the arrival of a possible angel is greeted with mockery and disrespect.

The movie begins with a night-time hurricane that rains down living crabs. A poor, farm couple discover a bedraggled and injured angel floundering in the water on the Columbian seashore. They give him shelter overnight in a chicken coop, but it is more like a prison. The young man even ropes him to a stake so that he can't escape.

The next day the word spreads among the villagers. They arrive out of curiosity, but all they see is a very old man with wings which may or may not be real. The young couple chase them outside their yard, and they must gawk at the spectacle from over the fence.

As the news spreads among the villagers, the priest comes to take a look. He announces that it's all a fraud. But some of the devout still believe. They camp out and surround the area with lit candles.

However, many of the villagers simply treat the spectacle as a joke. They throw garbage at the old man, teasing and taunting him like schoolboys. The crowd attracts vendors and hustlers. The event becomes a carnival for those with nothing better to do.

Meanwhile, the young couple have seen the old man naked and without his wings (they are detachable). The couple shield him from view, allowing him to appear in public only when he has put them back on.

Is he, or is he not, an angel? Is he a prankster, a demented old man? He never speaks. One can only judge by his effect. The young woman suspects he's an angel because her baby, who had a fever, got well when he arrived.

In another instance, people cry out that the angel is dead because he remains motionless. Three men enter the chicken coop with a branding iron and press it to his body. The old man leaps up, fully alive, but is whirling around from the pain. His massive, twirling wings cause a miniature tornado. Even a guitar is plucked up and spun off into the air. The evidence for his authenticity is growing.

The young couple know they've been blessed with good fortune, and they're willing to capitalize to the max. They charge an entrance fee to see the angel. Crowds from all over the countryside flock to take part. Parades. Live music. People in masquerade. The festival is non-stop, day and night.

Meanwhile, the priest is waging war against this heresy. He writes fake letters from the Vatican, attempting to undermine the credulity of the ignorant peasants.

As the angelic event persists, it grows into an amusement park replete with cotton candy, Ferris wheels, merry-go-rounds, lotteries, burlesque shows, and even a freak show of "The Spider Woman" who was transformed into a spider for disobeying her parents. The crowds keep growing, attracting visitors from all over South America.

Eventually, the party is over. People become bored and go home. After six years, the old man is even more debilitated. He crawls around the small hovel and gets in the couple's way. The woman, now middle-aged, says she wishes he would die. When she is alone, she has a heavenly vision of angels and regrets what she had said.

But the very old man takes his cue. He plucks the feathers off geese and uses them to repair his old, tattered wings. The young couple's baby, now a little six-year-old boy, says the angel is going to fly.

The next day "The Very Old Man with Enormous Wings" takes to the air. A few of the neighbors (mostly children) witness the miracle, but the majority, even of the faithful, are no longer there. After all, it's been six years. Who can wait that long, even for a miracle?

Director Fernando Birri and author Gabriel Garcia Marquez have created a visual feast of magical realism for the senses, a parody of man's lack of faith, and of his commercialization of the divine. If Christ were to return, would he be recognized or scoffed at? Would Buddha be honored or laughed out of town? More than likely they would be stoned, or simply ignored. And even if recognized, in what manner would they preach? At the Astrodome for tickets costing hundreds of dollars? Giving weekend seminars for a mere few thousand bucks? If the divine is really divine, perhaps they would simply put on a pair of wings and fly off into the blue sky.

WAKING LIFE

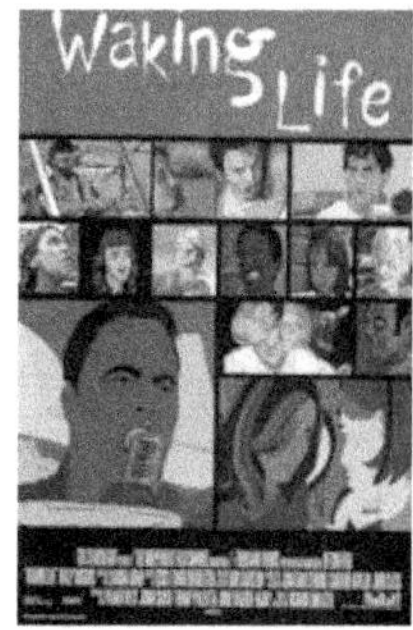

Director: Richard Linklater
Producer: Anne Walker-McBay, Tommy Pallotta, Palmer West & Jonah Smith
Screenplay: Richard Linklater
2001 Color

The Tibetan yogis believe that when we die, we pass into a realm of continual dreams. They have even developed a "yoga of dreams" so as to become aware that one is dreaming while still asleep. Through these "lucid" dreams one can gain control over one's consciousness, over the dream itself, and thus over one's destiny in the afterlife. It is practice, a mock-run, for what we will experience at death. For if we can remain conscious in our dreams, then so too will we maintain conscious awareness in the afterlife. We will not be lost and adrift in a phantasmagoria of illusions when we die.

Waking Life is a profound film of Tibetan Buddhistic enlightenment. Director/writer Richard Linklater may feign simple philosophic dialogue and artistic flair as his theme. But the dream-reality dichotomy runs central to the movie's structure, as well as to its motif and plot.

Linklater employs a unique process known as rotoscoping for filming and creating his movie. Live actors and real scenery are filmed on digital video. Then different artists digitally paint over the film footage to create the animation effect. Linklater used different artists for different characters and scenes to give a diverse, mosaic appearance to his film. His approach is ingenious. The movie vibrates with colorful energy. One never becomes rutted in a certain look or perspective. The screen is alive, more so than with any real-life footage.

The movie begins with a seemingly innocuous children's word and number game. A small boy and girl are playing on a door stoop. The boy's fortune is unraveled by the little girl: "Dream is destiny." The portentous message sends the boy floating off in a lucid dream.

In the next scene a young man (Wiley Wiggins playing his animated self) is returning to his home town by train. He awakens from his dream or reverie of childhood. He is the little boy now grown to college age. As Wiley wanders around town, he crosses paths with fate. A piece of paper lies conspicuously in the middle of the street. He bends down and unfolds it: "Look to your right." He does so, and sees a car barreling down. Wiley wakes up in bed. It was only a dream.

Wiley continues his meandering quest from where the dream left off. He has interesting encounters with many colorful characters. Their philosophical conversations are intense—ranging from existentialism to the evolution of man, to the nature of language, to the metaphysics of reincarnation. He absorbs it all like a sponge until something strange begins to happen. Wiley suspects that his supposed waking life is just another dream. He can't seem to really wake up. One tip-off that he's dreaming is that digital numbers on clocks and watches seem to waver and blur. He can't make them out. He now has reasons to ask questions.

One place Wiley gets answers is in a coffee house (a "Cafe of Dreams?"). Several oneironauts (explorers of dreams) expound upon the nature of his problem. One even paraphrases Havelock Ellis: "You know, they say that dreams are real only as long as they last. Couldn't you say the same thing about life?" He then goes on to discourse on the dream-reality dichotomy:

> "To the functional system of neural activity that creates our world, there is no difference between dreaming a perception and an action, and actually the waking perception and action."

The words are ominous and foreboding. To our brain and mind, there is really no difference between being awake and dreaming, especially if you are dreaming that you are awake, which is Wiley's problem.

Another oneironaut, playing a ukulele, gives valuable insight into what Wiley must do: "The trick is to combine your waking rational abilities with the infinite possibilities of your dreams. Cause if you can do that, you can do anything."

And finally, the last of the three holy oneironauts, in the Cafe of Dreams, gives the most practical advice on Wiley's dilemma:

> "But the trick is, you gotta realize that you're dreaming in the first place. You gotta be able to recognize it. You gotta be able to ask yourself, 'Hey man, is this a dream?' See, most people never ask themselves that when they're awake, or especially when they're asleep. Seems like everyone's sleep-walking through their waking state or wake-walking through their dreams. Either way, they're not going to get much out of it."

He then explains that another clue to becoming lucid, besides digital numbers wavering, is the inability to read small print. But the best telltale giveaway is the inability to adjust light levels, even when you are lucid. "You can't really do that . . . That's one of the few things you can't do in a lucid dream."

In an ironic conclusion to this lucid meeting in the Cafe of Dreams, Wiley rises from his table and walks to the door. He sees a light switch and flippantly decides to flip off the switch. Nothing happens. The lighting remains the same. He flips it on and off several times and nothing happens. An ominous feeling courses through him as he looks back to his dream advisor. The third oneironaut sits at the table, and with a sheepish grin he shrugs his shoulders.

Wiley realizes, ironically, that he's been dreaming that he's been talking about dreams. When full lucidity arrives he begins to levitate, and then ethereally floats out the window. All that he has been experiencing has been a dream—a dream interrupted by false-awakenings and moments of lucidity. He has now raised his awareness to full consciousness that he is dreaming. He is fully awake in his dream. And now all he wants is to wake up in real life. But he can't. He is still a prisoner in his own mind.

Wiley's further dream adventures lead him to an encounter with the "Ant-Girl." She is dismayed by our inhuman, alienated culture. We run around like ants or robots, not really connecting as human beings. Wiley is fascinated by her thoughts and creative insights (he certainly never had such ideas on his own). But he is also intrigued by the notion that she is just a figment of his imagination.

" . . . what's it like to be a character in a dream?" he challenges her very being.

But the Ant-Girl is quick to counter: "So, what about you?

What's your name? What's your address? What are you doing?"

She has him there. For in a dream, even a lucid one, facts and figures are difficult to recall.

"I can't remember right now. . . . .

But that's beside the point—whether I can dredge up this information . . ."

Wiley is being disingenuous, although he feels justified in his position. But the viewer realizes his logic doesn't cut it. It isn't consistent. For if he admonishes the Ant-Girl for being just a character in his dream with no personal reality of her own, then her challenge to him is equally valid and unsettling. Why can't he remember something as simple as his address, or his mother's maiden name? Perhaps he, himself, is also nothing but a dream character. Hence, his air of superiority is unfounded.

A tacit truce is upheld: I won't challenge your existence if you don't challenge mine. And Wiley goes on to comment on the nature of this epic dream, which may be a shared dream.

"It's not like I'm having a bad dream. It's a great dream. But, it's so unlike any other dream I've ever had before. It's like 'The Dream.' It's like I'm being prepared for something."

The following scene, where Wiley talks to a man on a bridge, seems to add validity to the Ant-Girl's position. It is similar to Jorge Luis Borges' story of "The Other" in which fictional characters dream each other into existence. "As one realizes that one is a dream figure in another person's dream—that is self-awareness."

But if Wiley is simply another dream character, then who is the dreamer—God? Perhaps. The Tibetan Buddhists might claim so.

Wiley gains more pieces to his enlightenment puzzle through, of all things, television. As he flips through the channels he happens upon a woman discoursing on dreams, death, and the afterlife:

> "Down through the centuries the notion that life is wrapped in a dream has been a pervasive theme of philosophers and poets. So doesn't it make sense that death, too, would be wrapped in a dream?—that after death your conscious life would continue in what might be called a dream body? It would be the same dream body you experience in your everyday dream life except that in the post-mortal state you could never again wake up, never again return to your physical body."

Is Wiley really dead? The awareness is dawning. Is he in the afterlife state which is akin to a dream? Did he actually die at the beginning of the film when he got run over by a car? Was his awakening in bed, merely an awakening to the afterlife?

Questions abound. In his last ontological conversation he speaks with the "Pinball Guy":

> "I keep waking up . . . but I'm just waking up into another dream. And I'm starting to get creeped out, too, like I'm talking to dead people. This woman on TV's telling me about how death is this dreamtime that exists outside of life. I mean, I'm starting to think that I'm dead."

The Pinball Guy tells his own fascinating dream. But Wiley will not be sidetracked. He persists in finding a way out of his metaphysical labyrinth:

> "I keep thinking that I'm waking up, but I'm still in a dream. It seems like it's going on forever. I can't get out of it. And I want to wake up for real. How do you really wake up?"

The scene ends with the Pinball Guy waving his hand, and magically intoning "wake up." Wiley suddenly wakes up—to reality? He gets out of bed, walks down the street, and returns to his old childhood home. It is the home from the first scene of the movie where the little boy and girl are playing word games on the front stoop. "Dream is destiny" was our young dreamer's fortune. And just like at the beginning when the little boy started to float upward by the car—so too does his older and wiser incarnation. Wiley's legs float back. He tries to grab the car door handle, but misses. He then drifts and soars upward, fully aware of The Dream—a heavenly image of Buddhistic transcendence as he disappears into the blue.

Director/writer Richard Linklater has created a fascinating movie of Buddhistic enlightenment. A difficult, perhaps nearly impossible concept to convey, is delivered in a visually stunning array of images and mind-boggling conversations. If our life is but a dream, then when we awaken at death, we may be greeted by a world not unlike that of Waking Life—a sobering thought which may prompt one to learn the Tibetan yoga of dreams—a thought which may make one more conscious of one's "Waking Life."

If life is akin to a dream, then Linklater's movie may be a fair approximation of transcendence. One wonders if a more apt title might be Waking Dream or, even better, Dreaming life.

AFTERWORD

At sixteen I had a dream that was the answer to my vision quest. It occurred during that crucial period when self-consciousness and "self"-seeking were all that mattered.

The dream was on a grand scale: an action-packed epic that encompassed all of life. There was war; there was love; there was death, fear, and anguish. It was drama on a cosmic scale. But it was also an incredible work of art.

At the end of the dream, there were festivities and celebration. The production was a success. It was like the end of a grand performance. The actors and actresses were making their curtain calls. People were partying and commending each other's role. Heroes and villains were together as friends. It was, after all, only a performance. But it was a successful production—one of the best movies of all time.

I realized, after I awoke, that the dream was a metaphor for life. After all we've gone through, the play will one day end. The stage props will be dismantled. One's fellow-actors will depart.

I vowed, then and there, to write a novel about life being analogous to an incredibly long movie. What happens, how it ends, the plot and characterization, depending solely upon the players and actors involved.

Now that I am fifty-five, I realize how much truth was revealed in that adolescent dream. While the novel has not yet been written, the camera nevertheless rolls on—cannot help but roll on. And it will continue to roll on till the final "cut." And when that moment arrives I am certain that champagne corks will pop, and the festivities will begin. Friends and long-lost loved ones will be congratulating each other on a great show.

Wayne Omura

www.ingramcontent.com/pod-product-compliance
Lightning Source LLC
LaVergne TN
LVHW050535100826
845148LV00002B/561